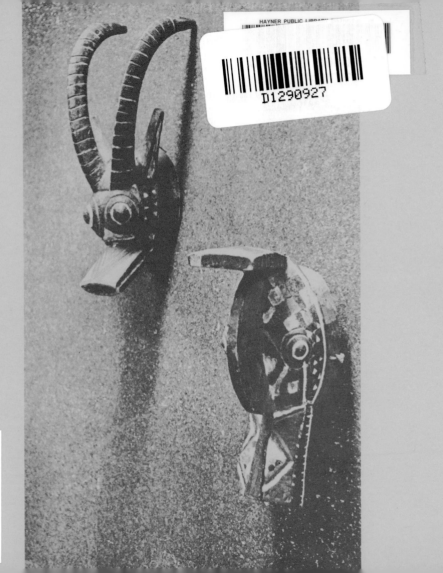

NAMES
from
AFRICA

Their Origin, Meaning, and Pronunciation

NAMES from

AFRICA

Their Origin, Meaning, and Pronunciation

By Ogonna Chuks-orji

Edited and with a Commentary by Keith E. Baird

 JOHNSON PUBLISHING COMPANY INC.   CHICAGO, 1972

Grateful acknowledgement is made to my
family and friends in Nigeria, and to
many African students who helped in the
preparation of the manuscript.
Ogonna Chuks-orji

Copyright 1972 by **JOHNSON PUBLISHING CO. INC.**

All rights reserved including the right to reproduce
this book or portion thereof in any form.

Library of Congress Catalog Card No. 72-154523
ISBN No. 0-87485-046-0

Printed in the United States of America

Design and photography by Norman L. Hunter

**Photographs of African art from the
Johnson Publishing Company collection.**

Contents

To Mom, Dad, and
      Brother Ejimofor Chuks-orji

Preface

This book has been written for people of all ages. Parents will use the book to find names for their children, but any individual of any age can take an African name to substitute for or add to his given name. Students in Black Studies programs may want to adopt a name that is meaningful to them.

I undertook this collection as a result of numerous inquiries for African names from many people in all walks of life who were interested in using them for themselves, their children, and their friends.

The giving of names is of great importance in Africa. People are named after events, happenings, great things, the days of the week, or the order in which they were born. For example, if a couple had long wanted a son, in Nigeria they may call him "Ayinde" (Yoruba), meaning the one we prayed for. In Ghana, if a boy is born on Saturday he is called "Kwame" (Akan). In Tanzania, the second born of twins will be called "Doto" (Zaramo). People have asked me whether names like James, Gary, or Francis could be translated into African form. There is no direct translation from English names to African, but if we go back to the original meaning of an English name, we can often find an African equivalent. For example, the English Theodore and the Ibo "Okechuku" both mean "God's gift."

I hope that each individual will find in this book a name to like, whose meaning will be appropriate and "a good fit."

Ogonna Chuks-orji
Oakland, 1972

1

NAMES from AFRICA:

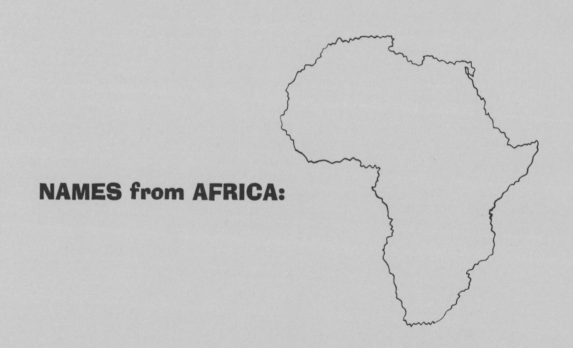

FEMALE

Name	Pronunciation	Meaning	Language and Country
Aba	*ah-BAH*	born on Thursday	Fante, Ghana
Ababuo	*ah-bah-BOO-oh*	child that keeps coming back	Ewe, Ghana
Abagbe	*AH-bah-beh*	we begged to have this one to lift up	Yoruba, Nigeria
Abam	*ah-BAHM*	second child after twins	Twi, Ghana
Abayomi	*ah-BAH-yoh-mee*	pleasant meeting	Yoruba, Nigeria
Abbo	*AH-boh*	vegetable	Mudama, Uganda
Abebi	*AH-beh-BEE*	we asked for her (and got her)	Yoruba, Nigeria
Abeje	*ah-beh-JEH*	we asked to have this one	Yoruba, Nigeria
Abeke	*ah-beh-KEH*	we begged for her to pet her	Yoruba, Nigeria
Abena	*ah-beh-NAH*	born on Tuesday	Fante, Ghana
Abeni	*ah-beh-NEE*	we asked for her, and behold she is ours!	Yoruba, Nigeria
Abeo	*ah-beh-OH*	her birth brings happiness	Yoruba, Nigeria
Abidemi	*ah-bee-deh-MEE*	born during father's absence	Yoruba, Nigeria
Abikanile	*ah-bee-kah-NEE-leh*	listen	Yao, Malawi
Abimbola	*ah-BEEM-boh-lah*	born to be rich	Yoruba, Nigeria

Note: asterisks indicate references in the Commentary.

Name	Pronunciation	Meaning	Language and Country
Adebola	*ah-DEH-boh-lah*	comer met honor	Yoruba, Nigeria
Adebomi	*ah-deh-bon-MEE*	crown covered my nakedness	Yoruba, Nigeria
Adedagbo	*ah-DEH-dah-boh*	happiness is a crown	Yoruba, Nigeria
Adedewe	*ah-DEH-deh-weh*	the crown is shattered	Yoruba, Nigeria
Adedoja	*ah-DEH-doh-jah*	crown becomes a thing of worth	Yoruba, Nigeria
Adeleke	*ah-DEH-leh-keh*	crown achieves happiness	Yoruba, Nigeria
Adeola	*ah-deh-oh-LAH*	crown has honor	Yoruba, Nigeria
Aderinola	*ah-DEH-ree-noh-lah*	crown walked toward wealth	Yoruba, Nigeria
Adesimbo	*ah-deh-SEEM-boh*	noble birth	Yoruba, Nigeria
Adowa	*ah-doh-WAH*	born on a Tuesday	Akan, Ghana
Aduke	*ah-doo-KEH*	much loved	Yoruba, Nigeria
Adwoa	*ah-dwoh-AH*	born on a Monday	Fante, Ghana
Afafa	*ah-FAH-fah*	first child of second husband	Ewe, Ghana
Afiya	*ah-FEE-yah*	health	Swahili, Tanzania
Afryea	*ah-FRY-yah*	born during good times	Ewe, Ghana

Name	Pronunciation	Meaning	Language and Country
Afua	*ah-FOO-ah*	born on Friday	Ewe, Ghana
Ain	*ah-EEN*	eye, hence "precious"	Arabic, N. Africa
Aina	*ah-ee-NAH*	delivery had complications [umbilical cord twisted around neck]	Yoruba, Nigeria
Aisha	*ah-EE-shah*	life	Swahili, E. Africa
Aiyetoro	*ah-YEH-toh-roh*	peace on earth	Yoruba, Nigeria
Akanke	*ah-kahn-KEH*	to meet her is to love her	Yoruba, Nigeria
Akilah	*AH-kee-lah*	intelligent, one who reasons	Arabic, N. Africa
Akosua	*ah-KOH-soo-ah*	born on Sunday	Ewe, Ghana
Akua	*ah-KOO-ah*	born on Wednesday	Ewe, Ghana
Akwete	*ah-KWEH-teh*	elder of twins	Ga, Ghana
Akwokwo	*ah-KWO-kwoh*	younger of twins	Ga, Ghana
Alaba	*ah-lah-BAH*	second child born after twins	Yoruba, Nigeria
Alake	*ah-lah-KEH*	one to be petted and made much of	Yoruba, Nigeria
Alile	*ah-LEE-leh*	she weeps	Yao, Malawi
Aluna	*ah-LOO-nah*	come here	Mwera, Kenya

Name	Pronunciation	Meaning	Language and Country
Ama	*AH-mah*	born on Saturday	Ewe, Ghana
Amadi	*ah-MAH-dee*	general rejoicing	Ibo, Nigeria
Aminah	*ah-MEE-nah*	honest, faithful [mother of Muhammad Ib'n Abdullah]	Arabic, N. Africa
Amonke	*ah-mohn-KEH*	to know her is to pet her	Yoruba, Nigeria
Antobam	*ahn-toh-BAHM*	posthumous child	Fante, Ghana
Arusi [*or* Harusi]	*ah-ROO-see*	born at the time of a wedding	Swahili, E. Africa
Asabi	*ah-sah-BEE*	she is of choice birth	Yoruba, Nigeria
Asale	*ah-SAH-leh*	speak	Yao, Malawi
Asha	*AH-shah*	life	Swahili, E. Africa
Ashura	*ah-SHOO-rah*	born during Islamic month Ashur	Swahili, E. Africa
Asya	*AHSS-yah*	born at a time of grief	Swahili, E. Africa
Ayo*	*AH-yoh*	joy	Yoruba, Nigeria
Ayobami	*ah-yoh-BAH-mee*	I am blessed with joy	Yoruba, Nigeria
Ayobunmi	*ah-yoh-BOON-mee*	joy is given to me	Yoruba, Nigeria
Ayodele*	*ah-yoh-DEH-leh*	joy comes home	Yoruba, Nigeria

Name	Pronunciation	Meaning	Language and Country
Ayofemi	*ah-yoh-FEH-mee*	joy likes me	Yoruba, Nigeria
Ayoluwa	*ah-yoh-LOO-wah*	joy of our people	Yoruba, Nigeria
Ayoola	*Ah-YOH-oh-lah*	joy in wealth	Yoruba, Nigeria
Aziza	*ah-ZEE-zah*	precious	Swahili, E. Africa
Baba	*BAH-bah*	born on Thursday	Fante, Ghana
Baderinwa	*bah-day-REEN-wah*	worthy of respect	Yoruba, Nigeria
Bahati	*bah-HAH-tee*	luck	Swahili, E. Africa
Bayo	*BAH-yoh*	joy is found	Yoruba, Nigeria
Bejide	*beh-JEE-deh*	child born in the rainy time	Yoruba, Nigeria
Bimkubwa	*beem-KOOB-wah*	a great lady	Swahili, E. Africa
Boahinmaa	*bwa-HIN-mah*	one who has left her own community, expatriate	Ewe, Ghana
Bolade	*BOH-lah-deh*	honor arrives	Yoruba, Nigeria
Bolanile	*baw-lah-NEE-leh*	the wealth of this house	Yoruba, Nigeria
Bunmi	*BOON-mee*	my gift	Yoruba, Nigeria
Bupe	*BOO-peh*	hospitality	Nyakyusa, Tanzania

Name	Pronunciation	Meaning	Language and Country
Buseje	*boo-SEH-jeh*	ask me	Yao, Malawi
Chaonaine	*chah-oh-nah-EE-neh*	it has seen me	Ngoni, Malawi
Chausiku	*chah-oo-SEE-koo*	born at night	Swahili, E. Africa
Chemwapuwa	*chem-WAH-poo-wah*	that which you are given	Shona, Zimbabwe
Chiku	*CHEE-koo*	chatterer	Swahili, E. Africa
Chimwala	*cheem-WAH-lah*	stone	Yao, Malawi
Chinue	*CHEEN-weh*	God's own blessing	Ibo, Nigeria
Chipo	*CHEE-poh*	gift	Shona, Zimbabwe
Chiwa	*CHEE-wah*	death	Yao, Malawi
Chotsani*	*chot-SAH-nee*	take away	Yao, Malawi
Chuki*	*CHOO-kee*	born when there was animosity	Swahili, N. Africa
Dada	*DAH-dah*	child with curly hair	Yoruba, Nigeria
Dalila	*dah-LEE-lah*	gentle	Swahili, E. Africa
Dalili	*dah-LEE-lee*	sign, omen	Swahili, E. Africa
Dayo	*DAH-yoh*	joy arrives	Yoruba, Nigeria

Name	Pronunciation	Meaning	Language and Country
Dikeledi	*dee-KEH-leh-dee*	tears	Tswana, Botswana
Do	*doh*	first child after twins	Ewe, Ghana
Dofi	*DOH-fee*	second child after twins	Ewe, Ghana
Doto	*DOH-toh*	second of twins	Zaramo, Tanzania
Dziko	*ZEE-koh*	the world	Nguni, S. Africa
Ebun	*eh-BOON*	gift	Yoruba, Nigeria
Edenausegboye	*eh-deh-nah-oo-seh-BOH-yeh*	good deeds are remembered	Benin, Nigeria
Efia	*eh-FEE-ah*	born on Friday	Fante, Ghana
Ekaghogho	*eh-kah-HO-hoh*	born on an important day	Benin, Nigeria
Emojung	*EH-moh-yong*	the old one	Karamojong, Uganda
Enomwoyi	*eh-nohm-WOH-yee*	one who has grace, charm	Benin, Nigeria
Enyonyam	*EN-yo-nam*	it is good for me	Ewe, Ghana
Eshe	*EH-sheh*	life	Swahili, E. Africa
Esi	*eh-SEE*	born on Sunday	Fante, Ghana
Fabayo	*fah-BAH-yoh*	a lucky birth is joy	Yoruba, Nigeria

Name	Pronunciation	Meaning	Language and Country
Faizah	*FAH-ee-zah*	victorious	Arabic, N. Africa
Fatima	*FAH-tee-mah*	daughter of the Prophet	Arabic, N. Africa
Fatuma	*fah-TOO-mah*	weaned [name of the daughter of the Prophet Muhammad]	Swahili, E. Africa
Fayola	*fah-YOH-lah*	good fortune walks with honor	Yoruba, Nigeria
Femi	*FEH-mee*	love me	Yoruba, Nigeria
Fola	*FAW-lah*	honor	Yoruba, Nigeria
Folade	*faw-lah-DEH*	honor arrives	Yoruba, Nigeria
Folami	*faw-LAH-mee*	respect and honor me	Yoruba, Nigeria
Folashade	*faw-lah-shah-DEH*	honor confers a crown	Yoruba, Nigeria
Folayan	*faw-LAH-yahn*	to walk in dignity	Yoruba, Nigeria
Foluke	*foh-LOO-keh*	placed in God's care	Yoruba, Nigeria
Fujo	*FOO-joh*	born after parents' separation	Swahili, E. Africa
Fukayna	*foo-KEH-ee-nah*	knowledgeable, scholarly	Arabic, N. Africa
Goitsemedime	*khoat-say-moh-DEE-meh*	God knows	Tswana, Botswana
Habibah	*hah-BEE-bah*	beloved	Arabic, N. Africa

Name	Pronunciation	Meaning	Language and Country
Hadiya	*hah-DEE-yah*	gift	Swahili, E. Africa
Hafsah	*HAF-sah*	wife of the Prophet	Arabic, N. Africa
Hafthah	*HAF-thah*	preserved, protected	Arabic, N. Africa
Halima	*hah-LEE-mah*	gentle	Swahili, E. Africa
Hanifah	*hah-NEE-fah*	true believer	Arabic, N. Africa
Haoniyao	*hah-oh-nee-YAH-oh*	born at the time of a quarrel [*lit.* he doesn't see his own faults]	Swahili, E. Africa
Haqikah	*hah-KEE-kah*	truthful	Arabic, N. Africa
Hasanati	*hah-sah-NAH-tee*	good	Swahili, E. Africa
Hasina	*hah-SEE-nah*	good	Swahili, E. Africa
Hawa*	*HAH-wah*	longing [also Eve]	Swahili, E. Africa
Hembadoon	*HEM-bah-doon*	the winner	Tiv, Nigeria
Husniyah	*hoos-NEE-yah*	beautiful	Arabic, N. Africa
Idowu	*ee-doh-WOO*	first child born after twins	Yoruba, Nigeria
Ifama	*ee-FAH-mah*	everything is fine	Ibo, Nigeria
Ife	*ee-FEH*	love	Yoruba, Nigeria

Name	Pronunciation	Meaning	Language and Country
Ifetayo	*ee-feh-TAH-yoh*	love brings happiness	Yoruba, Nigeria
Ige	*EE-geh*	delivered feet first	Yoruba, Nigeria
Ikuseghan	*ee-KOO-seh-han*	peace surpasses war	Benin, Nigeria
Irawagbon	*ee-rah-WAH-bon*	enemy's attempt to kill her	Benin, Nigeria
Isoke	*ee-SOH-keh*	a satisfying gift from God	Benin, Nigeria
Ityiarmbiamo	*ee-tee-arm-bee-AH-moh*	I am against wars	Tiv, Nigeria
Iverem	*ee-VEH-rem*	blessing and favor	Tiv, Nigeria
Iyabo	*ee-YAH-boh*	mother has returned	Yoruba, Nigeria
Izegbe	*ee-ZEH-beh*	long expected child	Benin, Nigeria
Jaha	*JAH-hah*	dignity	Swahili, E. Africa
Jamila	*jah-MEE-lah*	beautiful	Swahili, E. Africa
Japera	*jah-PEH-rah*	we are finished	Shona, Zimbabwe
Jendayi	*jen-DAH-yee*	give thanks	Shona, Zimbabwe
Jokha	*JOH-kah*	robe of adornment	Swahili, E. Africa
Jumapili	*joo-mah-PEE-lee*	born on Sunday	Mwera, Kenya

Name	Pronunciation	Meaning	Language and Country
Jumoke*	*joo–MOH–keh*	everyone loves the child	Yoruba, Nigeria
Kagiso	*kah–GHEE–soh*	peace	Tswana, Botswana
Kakra	*kah–KRAH*	younger of twins	Fante, Ghana
Kamaria	*kah–mah–REE–ah*	like the moon	Swahili, E. Africa
Kambo	*KAM–boh*	unlucky	Shona, Zimbabwe
Kamilah	*kah–MEE–lah*	the perfect one	Arabic, N. Africa
Kanika	*kah–NEE–kah*	black cloth	Mwera, Kenya
Kantayeni	*kan–tah–YAY–nee*	go and throw her away	Yao, Malawi
Karimah	*kah–REE–mah*	generous	Arabic, N. Africa
Kausiwa	*kah–oo–SEE–wah*	the poor	Yao, Malawi
Kehinde*	*keh–heen–DEH*	second born of twins	Yoruba, Nigeria
Kefilwe	*kay–FEEL–weh*	I am given	Tswana, Botswana
Kesi	*KEH–see*	born when father was in trouble	Swahili, E. Africa
Khadija	*kah–DEE–jah*	born prematurely [wife of the Prophet Muhammad]	Swahili, E. Africa
Kibibi	*kee–BEE–bee*	little lady	Swahili, E. Africa

Name	Pronunciation	Meaning	Language and Country
Kifimbo	*kee-FEEM-boh*	a very thin baby [*lit.* twig]	Swahili, E. Africa
Kijakazi	*kee-jah-KAH-zee*	your life is due to us	Swahili, E. Africa
Kissa	*kiss-SAH*	born after twins	Luganda, Uganda
Kizuwanda	*kee-zu-WAHN-dah*	last born child	Zaramo, Tanzania
Kokumo	*KOH-koo-moh*	this one will not die	Yoruba, Nigeria
Kukua	*koo-KOO-ah*	born on Wednesday	Fante, Ghana
Kuliraga	*koo-lee-RAH-gah*	weeping	Yao, Malawi
Kulwa	*KOOL-wah*	first of twins	Zaramo, Tanzania
Kunto	*KOON-toh*	third child	Twi, Ghana
Kwasausya	*kwa-sah-OOS-yah*	troubled	Yao, Malawi
Kyalamboka	*kee-ah-lam-BOH-kah*	God save me	Nyakyusa, Tanzania
Lateefah	*lah-TEE-fah*	gentle, pleasant	Arabic, N. Africa
Layla	*LAH-ee-lah*	born at night	Swahili, E. Africa
Lerato	*RAH-toh*	love	Tswana, Botswana
Limber	*LIM-ber*	joyfulness	Tiv, Nigeria

Name	*Pronunciation*	*Meaning*	*Language and Country*
Liziuzayani	*lee-zee-OO-zah-YAH-nee*	tell someone	Yao, Malawi
Lulu	*LOO-loo*	a pearl	Swahili, E. Africa
Lumusi	*loo-moo-SEE*	born face downwards	Ewe, Ghana
Mabuufo	*mah-BOO-foh*	troubles	Nguni, S. Africa
Mafuane	*mah-FOO-ah-neh*	soil	Bachopi, S. Africa
Maiba	*MAH-ee-bah*	grave	Shona, Zimbabwe
Maizah	*MAH-ee-zah*	discerning	Arabic, N. Africa
Mama	*mah-MAH*	born on Saturday	Fante, Ghana
Mandisa	*man-DEE-sah*	sweet	Xhosa, S. Africa
Mangeni	*man-GHEH-nee*	fish	Musamia, Uganda
Marjani	*mahr-JAH-nee*	coral	Swahili, E. Africa
Masani	*mah-SAH-nee*	has gap between teeth	Luganda, Uganda
Mashavu	*mah-SHAH-voo*	cheeks [*lit.* a baby with chubby cheeks]	Swahili, E. Africa
Masika	*mah-SEE-kah*	born during rainy season	Swahili, E. Africa
Maskini	*mah-SKEE-nee*	poor	Swahili, E. Africa

Name	Pronunciation	Meaning	Language and Country
Maulidi	*mah-oo-LEE-dee*	born during Islamic month Maulidi	Swahili, E. Africa
Mawiyah	*MAH-wee-yah*	the essence of life	Arabic, N. Africa
Mawusi	*mah-woo-SEE*	in the hands of God	Ewe, Ghana
Mbafor	*'m-BAH-fohr*	born on a market day	Ibo, Nigeria
Mbeke	*'m-beh-KEH*	born on the first day of the week	Ibo, Nigeria
Mesi	*MEH-see*	water	Yao, Malawi
Mhonum	*'m-HOH-num*	mercifulness	Tiv, Nigeria
Mkegani	*'m-keh-GAH-nee*	child of disrespectful wife	Zaramo, Tanzania
Mkiwa	*'m-KEE-wah*	orphaned child	Swahili, E. Africa
Modupe	*moh-DOO-peh*	I am grateful	Yoruba, Nigeria
Monifa	*MOH-nee-fah*	I have my luck	Yoruba, Nigeria
Montsho	*MOAN-shoh*	black	Tswana, Botswana
Morihinze	*moh-ree-hin-ZEH*	child of either sex is good	Tiv, Nigeria
Morowa	*moh-ROH-wah*	queen	Akan, Ghana
Mosi	*MOH-see*	the first-born	Swahili, E. Africa

Name	Pronunciation	Meaning	Language and Country
Moswen	*MOHSS-when*	white	Tswana, Botswana
Mpatuleni	*'m-pah-too-LAY-nee*	separate	Ngoni, Malawi
Mpho	*'m-POH*	gift	Tswana, Botswana
Msiba	*'m-SEE-bah*	born during calamity or mourning	Swahili, E. Africa
Mtupeni	*'m-too-PEH-nee*	not very welcome	Swahili, E. Africa
Mudiwa	*moo-DEE-wah*	beloved	Shona, Zimbabwe
Mukamutara	*moo-kah-moo-TAH-rah*	Mutara's daughter [i.e. born during the reign of King Mutara]	Rwanda, Rwanda
Mukantagara	*moo-kahn-tah-GAH-rah*	born in time of war	Rwanda, Rwanda
Mukarramma	*moo-kah-RAH-mah*	honored, respected	Arabic, N. Africa
Muminah	*MOO-mee-nah*	pious believer	Arabic, N. Africa
Mundufiki	*moon-doo-FEE-kee*	good for nothing	Nyakyusa, Tanzania
Munirah	*moo-NEE-rah*	one who enlightens	Arabic, N. Africa
Muslimah	*moose-LEE-mah*	devout believer	Arabic, N. Africa
Muteteli	*moo-tay-TAY-lee*	dainty	Rwanda, Rwanda
Muzwudzani	*mooz-woo-DZAH-nee*	whom should we tell	Shona, Zimbabwe

Name	Pronunciation	Meaning	Language and Country
Mwajuma	'm-wah-JOO-mah	born on Friday	Swahili, E. Africa
Mwaka	'm-WAH-kah	born during the opening of the farming year	Swahili, E. Africa
Mwamini	'm-wah-MEE-nee	honest	Swahili, E. Africa
Mwamuila	'm-wah-moo-EE-lah	born during the war	Zaramo, Tanzania
Mwanahamisi	'm-wah-nah-hah-MEE-see	born on Thursday	Swahili, E. Africa
Mwanaidi	'm-wah-nah-EE-dee	born during the Idd festival	Swahili, E. Africa
Mwanajuma	'm-wah-nah-JOO-mah	born on Friday	Swahili, E. Africa
Mwanakhamisi	'm-wah-nah-hah-MEE-see	born on Thursday	Swahili, E. Africa
Mwanatabu	'm-wah-nah-TAH-boo	born at time of trouble	Swahili, E. Africa
Mwanawa	'mwah-NAH-wah	first born child	Zaramo, Tanzania
Mwanjaa	'm-wah-nan-JAAH	born during famine	Zaramo, Tanzania
Mwasaa	'm-wa-SAH	timely	Swahili, E. Africa
Mwatabu*	'm-wah-TAH-boo	born at a time of sorrow	Swahili, E. Africa
Mwaurayeni	'mwah-OO-rah-YEH-nee	what have you killed?	Shona, Zimbabwe
Mwazwenyi	'mwaz-WEN-yee	what have you heard?	Shona, Zimbabwe

Name	Pronunciation	Meaning	Language and Country
Nabirye	*nah-beer-YEH*	one who produces twins	Luganda, Uganda
Nabukwasi	*nah-boo-KWAH-see*	bad housekeeper	Luganda, Uganda
Nabulungi	*nah-boo-long-GHEE*	beautiful one	Luganda, Uganda
Naeemah	*nah-EE-mah*	benevolent	Arabic, N. Africa
Nafula	*nah-foo-LAH*	born during rainy season	Abaluhya, Uganda
Nafuna	*nah-foo-NAH*	delivered feet first	Luganda, Uganda
Nailah	*NAH-ee-lah*	one who succeeds	Arabic, N. Africa
Nalongo	*nah-long-GOH*	mother of twins	Luganda, Uganda
Namono	*NAH-moh-noh*	younger of twins	Luganda, Uganda
Namusobiya	*nah-moo-so-BEE-yah*	one who has offended	Musoga, Uganda
Nanyamka	*nah-YAHM-kah*	God's gift	Ewe, Ghana
Nasiche	*nah-SEE-cheh*	born in the locust season	Musoga, Uganda
Nathifa	*nah-THEEF-ah*	clean, pure	Arabic, N. Africa
Nayo	*NAH-yoh*	we have joy	Yoruba, Nigeria
Ndachitanji	*n-dah-chee-TAN-jee*	what have I done?	Ngoni, Malawi

Name	Pronunciation	Meaning	Language and Country
Neema	*neh-EH-mah*	born during prosperous times	Swahili, E. Africa
Ngabile	*'n-gah-BEE-leh*	I have got it	Nyakyusa, Tanzania
Ngozi	*'n-GOH-zee*	blessing	Ibo, Nigeria
Ngulinga	*n-goo-LEENG-gah*	weeping	Ngoni, Malawi
Njemile	*n-jeh-MEE-leh*	upstanding	Yao, Malawi
Nkosazana	*'n-koh-sah-ZAH-nah*	princess	Xhosa, S. Africa
Nneka	*'n-NEH-kah*	her mother is prominent	Ibo, Nigeria
Nnenia	*'n-NEH-nee-ah*	her grandmothers look alike	Ibo, Nigeria
Nobanzi	*noh-BAN-zee*	width	Xhosa, S. Africa
Nomalanga	*noh-mah-LANG-gah*	sunny	Zulu, S. Africa
Nombeko	*nom-BEH-KOH*	respect	Xhosa, S. Africa
Nomble	*NOM-bleh*	beauty	Xhosa, S. Africa
Nomuula	*noh-MOO-lah*	rain	Xhosa, S. Africa
Nonyameko	*nong-ya-MEH-koh*	patience	Xhosa, S. Africa
Nourbese	*noor-BEH-seh*	a wonderful child	Benin, Nigeria

Name	Pronunciation	Meaning	Language and Country
Nuru	*NOO-roo*	in the daylight	Swahili, E. Africa
Nwakaego	*'n-wah-kah-EH-goh*	more important than money	Ibo, Nigeria
Nyankomago	*ng-yank-oh-MAH-goh*	second child after twins	Twi, Ghana
Nyiramahoro	*nee-yee-rah-mah-HO-roh*	peaceful	Rwanda, Rwanda
Ode	*oh-DEH*	born along the road	Benin, Nigeria
Olabisi	*oh-LAH-bee-see*	joy is multiplied	Yoruba, Nigeria
Olabunmi	*aw-lah-BOON-mee*	honor has rewarded me	Yoruba, Nigeria
Olaniyi	*oh-lah-NEE-yee*	there's glory in wealth	Yoruba, Nigeria
Olubayo	*oh-loo-BAH-yoh*	highest joy	Yoruba, Nigeria
Olubunmi	*oh-loo-BOON-mee*	this highest gift is mine	Yoruba, Nigeria
Olufemi	*oh-LOO-feh-mee*	God loves me	Yoruba, Nigeria
Olufunke	*oh-loo-FOON-keh*	God gives me to be loved	Yoruba, Nigeria
Olufunmilayo	*oh-loo-foon-mee-LAH-yoh*	God gives me joy	Yoruba, Nigeria
Oluremi	*oh-loo-REH-mee*	God consoles me	Yoruba, Nigeria
Omolara	*oh-MOH-lah-rah*	born at the right time	Benin, Nigeria

Name	Pronunciation	Meaning	Language and Country
Omorenomwara	*oh-moh-reh-nom-WAH-rah*	meant not to suffer	Benin, Nigeria
Omorose	*oh-moh-ROH-seh*	my beautiful child	Benin, Nigeria
Omosede	*oh-MOH-seh-deh*	a child counts more than a king	Benin, Nigeria
Omosupe	*oh-MOH-soo-peh*	a child is the most precious thing	Benin, Nigeria
Oni	*oh-NEE*	desired	Benin, Nigeria
Oni	*AW-nee*	born in a sacred abode	Yoruba, Nigeria
Osayiomwabo	*Oh-sah-yohm-WAH-boh*	God will help us	Benin, Nigeria
Oseye	*oh-SEH-yeh*	the happy one	Benin, Nigeria
Ozigbodi	*oh-ZEE-gboh-dee*	patience	Ewe, Ghana
Panya*	*PAHN-yah*	mouse (a tiny baby)	Swahili, E. Africa
Panyin	*pahn-YEEN*	elder of twins	Fante, Ghana
Pasua	*pah-SOO-ah*	born by Caesarean operation	Swahili, E. Africa
Pili	*PEE-lee*	the second born	Swahili, E. Africa
Qubilah	*KWUB-ee-lah*	concord	Arabic, N. Africa
Rabiah	*rah-BEE-ah*	spring	Arabic, N. Africa

Name	Pronunciation	Meaning	Language and Country
Radhiya	*rah–THEE–yah*	agreeable	Swahili, E. Africa
Ramla	*RAHM–lah*	predictor of the future	Swahili, E. Africa
Rashida	*rah–SHEE–dah*	righteous	Swahili, E. Africa
Raziya	*rah–ZEE–yah*	agreeable	Swahili, E. Africa
Rehema	*reh–HEH–mah*	compassion	Swahili, E. Africa
Rufaro	*roo–FAH–roh*	happiness	Shona, Zimbabwe
Rukiya	*roo–KEE–yah*	she rises on high	Swahili, E. Africa
Saada	*sah–AH–dah*	help	Swahili, E. Africa
Sabah	*sah–BAH*	morning	Arabic, N. Africa
Safiya	*sah–FEE–yah*	clear-minded, pure	Swahili, E. Africa
Sagirah	*SAH–ghee–rah*	little one	Arabic, N. Africa
Saidah	*sah–EE–dah*	happy, fortunate	Arabic, N. Africa
Salama	*sah–LAH–mah*	peace	Swahili, E. Africa
Salihah	*SAH–lee–hah*	correct, agreeable	Arabic, N. Africa
Salma	*SAHL–mah*	safe	Swahili, E. Africa

Name	Pronunciation	Meaning	Language and Country
Sangeya	*san-GEH-yah*	hate me	Shona, Zimbabwe
Sanura	*sah-NOO-rah*	kitten [*lit.* a baby who looks like a kitten]	Swahili, E. Africa
Sauda	*sah-OO-dah*	dark-complexioned	Swahili, E. Africa
Sekelaga*	*seh-keh-LAH-gah*	rejoice	Nyakyusa, Tanzania
Selma	*sehl-mah*	secure	Arabic, N. Africa
Serwa	*sair-WAH*	noble woman	Ewe, Ghana
Shani	*SHAH-nee*	marvellous	Swahili, E. Africa
Sharifa	*shah-REE-fah*	distinguished	Swahili, E. Africa
Shiminege	*shee-me-NEH-geh*	let's see the future	Tiv, Nigeria
Shoorai	*shoh-oh-RAH-ee*	broom	Shona, Zimbabwe
Shukura	*shoo-KOO-rah*	be grateful	Swahili, E. Africa
Sibongile*	*see-bon-ghee-LEH*	thanks	Ndebele, Zimbabwe
Siboniso	*see-boh-NEE-soh*	sign	Zulu, S. Africa
Sigele	*see-GEH-leh*	left	Ngoni, Malawi
Sigolwide	*see-gol-WEE-deh*	my ways are straight	Nyakyusa, Tanzania

Name	Pronunciation	Meaning	Language and Country
Sikambagila	*see–kam–bah–GHEE–lah*	it doesn't suit him	Nyakyusa, Tanzania
Sikudhani	*see–koo–THAH–nee*	a surprise, unusual	Swahili, E. Africa
Siphiwe	*see–PEE–weh*	we were given	Zulu, S. Africa
Sisi	*see–SEE*	born on a Sunday	Fante, Ghana
Sitembile	*see–tem–bee–LEH*	trust	Ndebele, Zimbabwe
Siti	*SEE–tee*	lady	Swahili, E. Africa
Siwatu	*see–WAH–too*	born during time of conflict with another group [*lit.* they are not people]	Swahili, E. Africa
Siwazuru	*see–wah–ZOO–ree*	as Siwatu, [*lit.* they are not good]	Swahili, E. Africa
Subira	*soo–BEE–rah*	patience rewarded	Swahili, E. Africa
Suhailah	*soo–HAH–ee–lah*	gentle, easy	Arabic, N. Africa
Sukutai	*soo–koo–TAH–ee*	squeeze	Shona, Zimbabwe
Suma	*SOO–mah*	ask	Nyakyusa, Tanzania
Syandene	*see–ahn–DEH–neh*	punctual	Nyakyusa, Tanzania
Taabu*	*tah–AH–boo*	troubles	Swahili, E. Africa
Tabia	*tah–BEE–ah*	talents	Swahili, E. Africa

Name	Pronunciation	Meaning	Language and Country
Tahirah	*TAH-hee-rah*	pure	Arabic, N. Africa
Taiwo*	*TAH-ee-woh*	first born of twins	Yoruba, Nigeria
Takiyah	*tah-KEE-yah*	pious, righteous	Arabic, N. Africa
Tale	*TAH-leh*	green	Tswana, Botswana
Talibah	*tah-LEE-bah*	seeker after knowledge	Arabic, N. Africa
Tatu	*TAH-too*	the third born	Swahili, E. Africa
Tawiah	*TAH-wee-ah*	first child after twins	Ga, Ghana
Teleza	*teh-LEH-zah*	slippery	Ngoni, Malawi
Thema	*TAY-mah*	queen	Akan, Ghana
Themba	*TEHM-bah*	trusted	Zulu, S. Africa
Thandiwe	*tan-DEE-weh*	loving one	Xhosa, S. Africa
Tidyanawo	*teed-yah-NAH-woh*	we shall both eat	Ngoni, Malawi
Tisaubiranji	*ti-sah-oo-boo-RAN-jee*	why such poverty?	Ngoni, Malawi
Tithandianasi	*tee-tan-dee-ah-NAH-see*	we'll be finished by relative	Ngoni, Malawi
Titilayo	*tee-tee-lah-YOH*	happiness is eternal	Yoruba, Nigeria

Name	Pronunciation	Meaning	Language and Country
Torkwase	*tor-kwah-SEH*	queen	Yoruba, Nigeria
Tulimbwelu	*too-lim-BWEH-loo*	we are in the light	Nyakyusa, Tanzania
Tulinagwe	*too-lee-NA-gweh*	God is with us	Nyakyusa, Tanzania
Tumpe	*TOOM-peh*	let us thank God	Nyakyusa, Tanzania
Tupokigwe	*too-poh-KEE-gweh*	we are safe	Nyakyusa, Tanzania
Tusajigwe	*too-SAH-jee-gweh*	we are blessed	Nyakyusa, Tanzania
Tuwalole	*too-wah-loh-LEH*	exemplary	Zaramo, Tanzania
Twaponilo	*too-ah-poh-nee-LOH*	we are saved	Nyakyusa, Tanzania
Uchefuna	*oo-cheh-foo-NAH*	I have my wits about me	Ibo, Nigeria
Umayma	*oo-MAH-ee-mah*	little mother	Arabic, N. Africa
Umm	*oom*	mother	Arabic, N. Africa
Urbi	*OOR-bee*	princess	Benin, Nigeria
Uwimana	*oo-wee-MAH-nah*	daughter of God	Rwanda, Rwanda
Walidah	*wah-LEE-dah*	new born	Arabic, N. Africa
Waseme	*wah-SEH-meh*	let them talk	Swahili, Tanzania

Name	Pronunciation	Meaning	Language and Country
Wesesa	*weh-seh-SAH*	careless	Musoga, Uganda
Yaa	*YAH-ah*	born on Thursday	Ewe, Ghana
Yahimba	*yah-him-BAH*	there is nothing like home	Tiv, Nigeria
Yaminah	*yah-MEE-nah*	right and proper	Arabic, N. Africa
Ye	*YEH-eh*	elder of twins	Ewe, Ghana
Yejide	*yeh-jee-DEH*	the image of her mother	Yoruba, Nigeria
Yetunde*	*yeh-TOON-deh*	mother comes back	Yoruba, Nigeria
Zahra	*ZAH-rah*	flower	Swahili, Tanzania
Zainabu*	*zah-ee-NAH-boo*	beautiful [eldest daughter of Muhammed]	Swahili, E. Africa
Zakiya	*zah-KEE-yah*	intelligent	Swahili, E. Africa
Zalika	*zah-LEE-kah*	well-born	Swahili, E. Africa
Zawadi	*zah-WAH-dee*	gift	Swahili, E. Africa
Zesiro	*ZEH-see-roh*	elder of twins	Luganda, Uganda
Zubaidah	*zoo-BAH-ee-dah*	excellent	Arabic, N. Africa
Zuwena	*zoo-WEH-nah*	good	Swahili, E. Africa

NAMES from AFRICA:

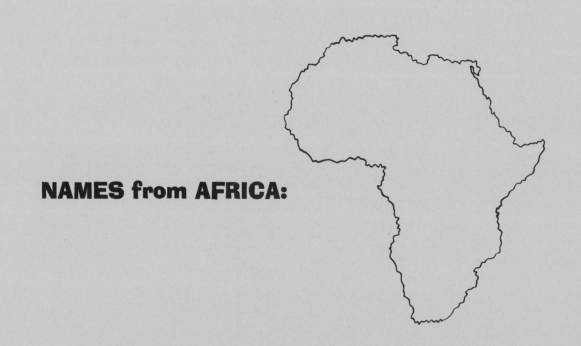

MALE

Name	Pronunciation	Meaning	Language and Country
Abasi	*ah-BAH-see*	stern	Swahili, E. Africa
Abayomi	*ah-BAH-yoh-mee*	born to bring me joy	Yoruba, Nigeria
Abdalla	*ab-DAHL-lah*	servant of God	Swahili, E. Africa
Abdu	*ab-DOO*	worshipper of God	Swahili, E. Africa
Abeeku	*ah-BAY-koo*	born on Wednesday	Fante, Ghana
Abegunde	*ah-beh-GOON-deh*	born during holiday	Yoruba, Nigeria
Abejide	*ah-beh-JEE-deh*	born during winter	Yoruba, Nigeria
Abiade	*ah-bee-ah-DEH*	born of royal parents	Yoruba, Nigeria
Abidugun	*ah-BEE-doo-goon*	born before the war	Yoruba, Nigeria
Abimbola	*ah-BEEM-boh-lah*	born rich	Yoruba, Nigeria
Abiodun	*ah-BEE-oh-doon*	born at the time of a festival	Yoruba, Nigeria
Abiola	*ah-BEE-oh-lah*	born in honor	Yoruba, Nigeria
Abiona	*ah-BEE-oh-nah*	born during a journey	Yoruba, Nigeria
Abioye	*ah-BEE-oh-yeh*	born during coronation	Yoruba, Nigeria
Abubakar	*ah-BOO-bah-kar*	noble	Swahili, E. Africa

Note: asterisks indicate references in the Commentary.

Name	Pronunciation	Meaning	Language and Country
Addae	*ah–DAH–eh*	morning sun	Akan, Ghana
Ade	*ah–DEH*	royal	Yoruba, Nigeria
Adeagbo	*ah–DEH–ag–boh*	he brings royal honor	Yoruba, Nigeria
Adebamgbe	*ah–DEH–bam–beh*	royalty dwells with me	Yoruba, Nigeria
Adebayo	*ah–DEH–bah–yoh*	he came in a joyful time	Yoruba, Nigeria
Adeben	*ah–deh–BEHN*	the twelfth born	Akan, Ghana
Adeboro	*ah–DEH–boh–roh*	royalty comes into wealth	Yoruba, Nigeria
Adedapo	*ah–DEH–dah–poh*	royalty brings the people together	Yoruba, Nigeria
Adegoke	*ah–DEH–goh–keh*	the crown has been exalted	Yoruba, Nigeria
Adejola	*ah–DEH–joh–lah*	the crown feeds on honors	Yoruba, Nigeria
Adelabu	*ah–DEH–lah–boo*	the crown passed through deep water	Yoruba, Nigeria
Adelaja	*ah–DEH–lah–jah*	the crown settles a quarrel	Yoruba, Nigeria
Ademola	*ah–DEH–moh–lah*	a crown is added to my wealth	Yoruba, Nigeria
Adesola	*ah–DEH–soh–lah*	the crown honored us	Yoruba, Nigeria
Adetokunbo	*ah–DEH–toh–koon–boh*	honor came from overseas	Yoruba, Nigeria

Name	Pronunciation	Meaning	Language and Country
Adewole	*ah-DEH-woh-leh*	royalty enters the house	Yoruba, Nigeria
Adeyemi	*ah-deh-yeh-MEE*	the crown suits me well	Yoruba, Nigeria
Adigun	*ah-dee-GOON*	righteous	Yoruba, Nigeria
Adika	*ah-dee-KAH*	first child of a second husband	Ewe, Ghana
Adio	*ah-dee-OH*	be righteous	Yoruba, Nigeria
Adisa	*ah-dee-SAH*	one who makes his meaning clear	Yoruba, Nigeria
Adofo	*ah-DOH-foh*	warrior	Akan, Ghana
Adom	*ah-DOHM*	help from God	Akan, Ghana
Adunbi	*ah-doon-BEE*	born to be pleasant	Yoruba, Nigeria
Adusa	*ah-DOO-sah*	thirteenth born	Akan, Ghana
Afiba	*ah-FEE-bah*	by the sea	Yoruba, Nigeria
Agyei	*ahd-JAY-ee*	messenger from God	Akan, Ghana
Agyeman	*ahd-JAY-man*	fourteenth born	Akan, Ghana
Agymah	*ahd-jee-MAH*	one who leaves his community, expatriate	Fante, Ghana
Ahmed	*ah-HMED*	praiseworthy	Swahili, E. Africa

Name	Pronunciation	Meaning	Language and Country
Aiyetoro	*ah-YEH-toh-roh*	peace on earth	Yoruba, Nigeria
Ajagbe	*ah-jahg-BEH*	he carries off the prize	Yoruba, Nigeria
Ajamu*	*ah-jah-MOO*	he fights for what he wants	Yoruba, Nigeria
Ajani	*ah-jah-NEE*	he fights for possession	Yoruba, Nigeria
Ajayi	*ah-JAH-yee*	born face-down	Yoruba, Nigeria
Akanni	*ah-KAHN-nee*	our encounter brings possessions	Yoruba, Nigeria
Akiiki	*ah-kee-EE-kee*	friend	Muneyankole, Uganda
Akil	*ah-KEEL*	intelligent, one who uses reason	Arabic, N. Africa
Akinkawon	*ah-keen-KAH-wohn*	bravery pacified them	Yoruba, Nigeria
Akinlabi	*ah-KEEN-lah-bee*	we have a boy	Yoruba, Nigeria
Akinlana	*ah-keen-LAH-nah*	valor	Yoruba, Nigeria
Akinlawon	*ah-keen-LAH-wohn*	bravery sustains them	Yoruba, Nigeria
Akins	*ah-KEENS*	brave boy	Yoruba, Nigeria
Akinsanya	*ah-KEEN-sahn-yah*	the hero avenges	Yoruba, Nigeria
Akinshegun	*ah-keen-sheh-GOON*	valor conquers	Yoruba, Nigeria

Name	Pronunciation	Meaning	Language and Country
Akinsheye	*ah-KEEN-sheh-yeh*	valor acts honorably	Yoruba, Nigeria
Akinshiju	*ah-KEEN-shee-joo*	valor awakes	Yoruba, Nigeria
Akintunde	*ah-KEEN-toon-deh*	a boy has come again	Yoruba, Nigeria
Akinwole	*ah-KEEN-woh-leh*	valor enters the house	Yoruba, Nigeria
Akinwunmi	*ah-KEEN-woon-mee*	valor is pleasing to me	Yoruba, Nigeria
Akinyele	*ah-keen-YEH-leh*	valor benefits this house	Yoruba, Nigeria
Akono	*ah-KOH-noh*	it is my turn	Yoruba, Nigeria
Akua	*a-KOO-ah*	born on Thursday	Fante, Ghana
Akwetee	*ah-KWAY-teh*	younger of twins	Ga, Ghana
Ali*	*ah-LEE*	exalted	Swahili, E. Africa
Alonge	*ah-LOHN-geh*	a tall and skinny boy	Yoruba, Nigeria
Amadi	*ah-MAH-dee*	seemed destined to die at birth	Benin, Nigeria
Ambakisye	*am-bah-KEES-yeh*	God has been merciful to me	Ndali, Tanzania
Ambidwile	*am-bee-DWEE-leh*	God has convinced me	Nyakyusa, Tanzania
Ambilikile	*am-bee-lee-KEE-leh*	God called me	Nyakyusa, Tanzania

Name	Pronunciation	Meaning	Language and Country
Ambokile	*am-bo-KEE-leh*	God has redeemed me	Nyakyusa, Tanzania
Ambonisye	*am-boh-NEES-yeh*	God has rewarded me	Nyakyusa, Tanzania
Ametefe	*ah-meh-teh-FEH*	child born after father's death	Ewe, Ghana
Ampah	*AHM-pah*	trust	Akan, Ghana
Anane	*ah-NAH-neh*	the fourth son	Akan, Ghana
Andalwisye	*ahn-dal-WEES-yeh*	God has shown me the way	Nyakyusa, Tanzania
Andengwisye	*ahn-deng-GWEES-yeh*	God has claimed me	Nyakyusa, Tanzania
Andongwisye	*ahn-dong-GWEES-yeh*	God has led me	Nyakyusa, Tanzania
Andwele	*ahn-DWEH-leh*	God brought me	Nyakyusa, Tanzania
Angolwisye	*ahn-gohl-WEES-yeh*	God has guided me	Nyakyusa, Tanzania
Angosisye	*ahn-goh-SEES-yeh*	God sanctified me	Nyakyusa, Tanzania
Animashaun	*AH-nee-mah-shohn*	generous	Yoruba, Nigeria
Ankoma	*ahn-KOH-mah*	last born of parents	Akan, Ghana
Anum	*AH-noom*	fifth born	Akan, Ghana
Anyabwile	*ahn-yah-BWEE-leh*	God has unchained me	Nyakyusa, Tanzania

Name	Pronunciation	Meaning	Language and Country
Anyelwiswe	*ahn-yel-WEES-weh*	God has purified me	Nyakyusa, Tanzania
Aondochimba	*ah-ohn-doh-HEEM-bah*	God is above all things on earth	Tiv, Nigeria
Apara	*ah-PAH-rah*	child that comes and goes	Yoruba, Nigeria
Ashur	*ah-SHOOR*	born during Islamic month Ashur	Swahili, Tanzania
Asim	*ah-SEEM*	protector, defender	Arabic, N. Africa
Asukile	*ah-soo-KEE-leh*	the Lord has washed me	Nyakyusa, Tanzania
Aswad	*ahss-WAHD*	black	Arabic, N. Africa
Ata	*ah-TAH*	twin	Fante, Ghana
Atsu	*at-SOO*	younger of twins	Ewe, Ghana
Atu	*ah-TOO*	born on Saturday	Fante, Ghana
Awotwe	*a-WOH-tweh*	eighth born	Akan, Ghana
Ayinde	*ah-yeen-DEH*	we gave praises and he came	Yoruba, Nigeria
Ayize	*Ah-YEE-zeh*	let it come	Zulu, S. Africa
Ayo*	*AH-yoh*	happiness	Yoruba, Nigeria
Ayodele*	*ah-YOH-deh-leh*	joy enters the house	Yoruba, Nigeria

Name	Pronunciation	Meaning	Language and Country
Ayubu	*ah–YOO–boo*	patience in suffering [*cf.* Job]	Swahili, E. Africa
Azagba	*ah–ZAH–bah*	born out of town	Benin, Nigeria
Azibo	*a–ZEE–boh*	earth	Ngoni, Malawi
Azikiwe	*ah–ZEE–kee–weh*	vigorous	Ibo, Nigeria
Azizi	*ah–ZEE–zee*	precious	Swahili, E. Africa
Babafemi	*bah–BAH–feh–mee*	father loves me	Yoruba, Nigeria
Babatunde*	*bah–bah–TOON–deh*	father returns	Yoruba, Nigeria
Babatunji	*bah–bah–TOON–jee*	father returns again	Yoruba, Nigeria
Badru	*BAH–droo*	born at full moon	Swahili, Tanzania
Badu	*bah–DOO*	tenth born	Akan, Ghana
Bakari	*bah–KAH–ree*	of noble promise	Swahili, E. Africa
Balogun	*bah–loh–GOON*	warlord	Yoruba, Nigeria
Balondemu	*bah–lon–DEH–moo*	chosen one	Musoga, Uganda
Bandele	*ban–DEH–leh*	born away from home	Yoruba, Nigeria
Banga	*BANG–gah*	knife	Shona, Zimbabwe

Name	Pronunciation	Meaning	Language and Country
Bangababo	*bah-ngah-BAH-boh*	discord in the family	Rwanda, Rwanda
Banjoko	*BAN-joh-koh*	stay with me and go no more	Yoruba, Nigeria
Bankole	*BAN-koh-leh*	help me to build the house	Yoruba, Nigeria
Baruti	*bah-ROO-tee*	teacher	Tswana, Botswana
Becktemba	*beck-tem-BAH*	to be trusted	Ndebele, Zimbabwe
Bem	*behm*	peace	Tiv, Nigeria
Beno	*BEH-noh*	one of a band	Mwera, Kenya
Betserai	*Beht-seh-RAH-ee*	help, assistance	Shona, Zimbabwe
Bilal	*bee-LAHL*	a black man, first convert of the Prophet Muhammad	Arabic, N. Africa
Bitalo	*bee-TAH-loh*	finger-licking	Luganda, Uganda
Bobo	*boh-BOH*	born on a Tuesday	Fante, Ghana
Bomani	*boh-MAH-nee*	warrior	Ngoni, Malawi
Boseda	*beh-SEH-deh*	born on a Sunday	Tiv, Nigeria
Bwagilo	*bwah-GHEE-loh*	source of things	Nyakyusa, Tanzania
Bwana Mkubwa	*bwah-nahm-KOOB-wah*	great master	Swahili, E. Africa

Name	Pronunciation	Meaning	Language and Country
Bwerani	*bweh-RAH-nee*	come (you are welcome)	Ngoni, Malawi
Chabwera*	*chah-BWEH-rah*	he has arrived	Ngoni, Malawi
Chafulumisa	*chah-foo-loo-MEE-sah*	swift	Ngoni, Malawi
Chatha	*CHAT-hah*	an ending	Ngoni, Malawi
Chatuluka	*chah-too-LOO-kah*	a departure	Ngoni, Malawi
Chekandino	*cheh-kan-DEE-noh*	spicy	Yao, Malawi
Chenzira	*chen-SEE-rah*	born on the road	Shona, Zimbabwe
Chibale	*chee-BAH-leh*	kinship	Ngoni, Malawi
Chigaru	*chee-GAH-roo*	hound	Ngoni, Malawi
Chihambuane	*chee-ham-boo-AH-neh*	sweet potatoes	Bachopi, S. Africa
Chijioke	*CHEE-jee-oh-keh*	God gives talent	Ibo, Nigeria
Chike	*CHEE-keh*	power of God	Ibo, Nigeria
Chikosi	*chee-KOH-see*	neck	Ngoni, Malawi
Chikumbu	*chee-KOOM-boo*	knife handle	Yao, Malawi
Chilemba	*chee-LEHM-bah*	turban	Mwera, Kenya

Name	Pronunciation	Meaning	Language and Country
Chimanga	*chee-MAHNG-gah*	maize	Ngoni, Malawi
Chimsima	*cheem-SEE-mah*	hard porridge	Ngoni, Malawi
Chinangwa	*chee-NANG-gwah*	cassava [an edible root]	Ngoni, Malawi
Chinelo	*CHEE-neh-loh*	thought of God	Ibo, Nigeria
Chinouyazue	*chee-noo-yah-ZWEH*	will be back again	Shona, Zimbabwe
Chinua	*CHEE-noo-ah*	God's own blessing	Ibo, Nigeria
Chioke	*CHEE-oh-keh*	gift of God	Ibo, Nigeria
Chionesu	*choh-NEH-soo*	guiding light	Shona, Zimbabwe
Chipita	*chee-PEE-tah*	it has gone	Ngoni, Malawi
Chisisi	*chee-SEE-see*	a secret	Yao, Malawi
Chisulo	*chee-SOO-loh*	steel	Yao, Malawi
Chitsime	*cheet-SEE-meh*	a well	Lomwe, Malawi
Chitundu	*chee-TOON-doo*	birds' nest	Mwera, Kenya
Chiumbo	*chee-OOM-boh*	small creation	Mwera, Kenya
Chiwanda	*chee-WAN-dah*	mad	Yao, Malawi

Name	Pronunciation	Meaning	Language and Country
Chiwocha	*chee-WOH-chah*	rooster	Lomwe, Malawi
Chuguel	*CHOO-goo-el*	sugar	Bachopi, S. Africa
Chukwueneka*	*choo-kwoo-eh-NEH-kah*	God has dealt kindly with us	Ibo, Nigeria
Chuma	*CHOO-mah*	wealth, beads	Shona, Zimbabwe
Chumachienda	*choo-mah-chee-EN-dah*	a dignitary is on his way, or . . . is travelling	Lomwe, Malawi
Citiwala	*chee-TWAH-lah*	insect	Yao, Malawi
Citseko	*cheet-SEH-koh*	door	Ngoni, Malawi
Coblah	*koh-BLAH*	born on Tuesday	Ewe, Ghana
Coffie	*koh-FEE*	born on Friday	Ewe, Ghana
Commie	*KOH-mee*	born on Saturday	Ewe, Ghana
Coujoe	*koh-JOH*	born on Monday	Ewe, Ghana
Dada	*DAH-dah*	child with curly hair	Yoruba, Nigeria
Dakarai	*dah-KAH-rah-ee*	happiness	Shona, Zimbabwe
Danjuma	*dan-joo-MAH*	born on Friday	Hausa, Nigeria
Danladi	*dan-LAH-dee*	born on Sunday	Hausa, Nigeria

Name	Pronunciation	Meaning	Language and Country
Darweshi	*dahr–WEH–shee*	saintly	Swahili, E. Africa
Daudi*	*dah–OO–dee*	beloved one	Swahili, E. Africa
Dawud	*dah–OOD*	beloved	Arabic, N. Africa
Dingane	*deen–GAH–neh*	a person in need	Zulu, S. Africa
Donkor	*dohn–KOR*	humble person	Akan, Ghana
Dukuzumuremyi	*doo–koo–zoo–moo–REM–yee*	praise be to God	Rwanda, Rwanda
Dulani	*doo–LAH–nee*	cutting	Ngoni, Malawi
Dumisai	*doo–mee–SAH–ee*	herald	Ndebele, Zimbabwe
Dunsimi	*doon–SEE–mee*	don't die before me	Yoruba, Nigeria
Durojaiye	*doo–roh–jah–YEH*	wait and enjoy what the world offers	Yoruba, Nigeria
Eberegbulam	*eh–BEH–reh–boo–lam*	my kindness shall not destroy me	Ibo, Nigeria
Ebo	*eh–BOH*	born on Tuesday	Fante, Ghana
Ehioze	*eh–HEE–oh–ZAY*	I am above people's jealousy	Benin, Nigeria
Ekundayo	*eh–KOON–dah–yoh*	sorrow becomes happiness	Yoruba, Nigeria
Enobakhare	*eh–noh–bah–KAH–reh*	the king's word	Benin, Nigeria

Name	Pronunciation	Meaning	Language and Country
Ewansiha	*eh–wan–see–HAH*	secrets are not for sale	Benin, Nigeria
Fadahunsi	*FAH–dah–hoon–see*	royalty has favored me	Arabic, N. Africa
Fadil	*FAH–deel*	generous	Arabic, N. Africa
Fakih	*fah–KEE*	legal expert; one who recites the Qu'ran	Arabic, N. Africa
Faraji	*fah–RAH–jee*	consolation	Swahili, E. Africa
Fenuku	*fay–noo–KOO*	born after term	Fante, Ghana
Fenyang	*fehn–YANG*	conqueror	Tswana, Botswana
Fifi	*fee–FEE*	born on Friday	Fante, Ghana
Foluke	*foh–LOO–keh*	placed in God's hands	Yoruba, Nigeria
Fudail	*foo–DAH–eel*	excellent in character	Arabic, N. Africa
Fulumirani	*foo–loo–mee–RAH–nee*	a journey	Ngoni, Malawi
Funsani	*foon–SAH–nee*	request	Ngoni, Malawi
Gahiji	*gah–HEE–jee*	the hunter	Rwanda, Rwanda
Gamba	*GAM–bah*	warrior	Shona, Zimbabwe
Garai	*GAH–rah–ee*	be settled	Shona, Rhodesia

Name	Pronunciation	Meaning	Language and Country
Goatsemodime	*Khoat–seh–moh–DEE–meh*	God knows	Tswana, Botswana
Gogo	*GOH–goh*	like grandfather	Nguni, S. Africa
Goredenna	*goh–reh–deh–NAH*	black cloud	Shona, Zimbabwe
Gowon	*GOH–wohn*	rainmaker	Tiv, Nigeria
Gwandoya	*gwan–DOH–yah*	met with misery	Luganda, Uganda
Gyasi	*JAH–see*	wonderful	Akan, Ghana
Habib	*hah–BEEB*	beloved	Arabic, N. Africa
Habimana	*ah–bee–MAH–nah*	God exists	Rwanda, Rwanda
Haji	*HAH–jee*	born during the month of pilgrimage to Mecca	Swahili, E. Africa
Hakizimana	*ah–kee–zee–MAH–nah*	it is God who saves	Rwanda, Rwanda
Hamadi	*hah–MAH–dee*	praised	Swahili, E. Africa
Hamidi	*hah–MEE–dee*	commendable	Swahili, E. Africa
Hamisi	*hah–MEE–see*	born on Thursday	Swahili, E. Africa
Hamza	*HAHM–zah*	historically significant personage	Arabic, N. Africa
Hanbal	*HAHN–bahl*	purity [founder of an Islamic school of thought]	Arabic, N. Africa

Name	Pronunciation	Meaning	Language and Country
Hanif	*HAH-neef*	true believer	Arabic, N. Africa
Haoniyao	*hah-oh-nee-YAH-oh*	born at the time of a quarrel [*lit.* he doesn't see his own faults]	Swahili, E. Africa
Harb	*harb*	war	Arabic, N. Africa
Harith	*HAH-reeth*	cultivator	Arabic, N. Africa
Harun	*hah-ROON*	exalted [*cf.* Hebrew: Aaron]	Arabic, N. Africa
Hasani	*hah-SAH-nee*	handsome	Swahili, E. Africa
Hashim	*HAH-sheem*	destroyer or crusher [of evil]	Arabic, N. Africa
Hondo	*HOHN-doh*	war	Shona, Zimbabwe
Husani [*var.* of Hasani]	*hoo-SAH-nee*	handsome	Swahili, E. Africa
Ibrahim	*EE-brah-heem*	my father is exalted	Hausa, Nigeria
Idi	*EE-dee*	born during Idd festival	Swahili, E. Africa
Idogbe	*ee-doh-BEH*	second born after twins	Yoruba, Nigeria
Idowu	*ee-DOH-woo*	born after twins	Yoruba, Nigeria
Imarogbe	*ee-MAH-roh-beh*	child born to a good family	Benin, Nigeria
Ipyana	*eep-YAH-nah*	grace	Nyakyusa, Tanzania

Name	Pronunciation	Meaning	Language and Country
Iroagbulam	*ee-ROH-eh-boo-lam*	let not enmity destroy me	Ibo, Nigeria
Ishaq	*EESS-hahk*	he laughs [*lit.* a child who laughed when he was born]	Arabic, N. Africa
Issa*	*ee-SAH*	God is our salvation	Swahili, E. Africa
Iyapo	*ee-YAH-po*	many trials	Yoruba, Nigeria
Jabari	*jah-BAH-ree*	brave	Swahili, E. Africa
Jabulani	*jah-boo-LAH-nee*	be happy	Ndebele, Zimbabwe
Jafari	*jah-FAH-ree*	creek	Swahili, E. Africa
Jahi	*JAH-hee*	dignity	Swahili, E. Africa
Jaja	*JAH-jah*	honored	Ibo, Nigeria
Jawhar	*jah-oo-HAR*	jewel; essence	Arabic, N. Africa
Jela	*JEH-lah*	father in prison at birth	Swahili, E. Africa
Jelani	*jeh-LAH-nee*	mighty	Swahili, E. Africa
Jibade	*jee-bah-DEH*	born close to royalty	Yoruba, Nigeria
Jibri	*jee-BREE*	archangel of Allah [*cf.* Hebrew: Gabriel]	Arabic, N. Africa
Jimiyu	*JEE-mee-yoo*	born in a dry season	Abaluhya, Uganda

Name	Pronunciation	Meaning	Language and Country
Jojo	*joh-JOH*	born on Monday	Fante, Ghana
Juma	*JOO-mah*	born on Friday	Swahili, E. Africa
Jumaane	*joo-MAH-neh*	born on Tuesday	Swahili, E. Africa
Jumoke*	*joo-MOH-keh*	everyone loves the child	Yoruba, Nigeria
Kadokechi	*kah-doh-KEH-chee*	bitter soup	Mudama, Uganda
Kafele	*kah-FEH-leh*	worth dieing for	Ngoni, Malawi
Kajakafwile	*kah-jah-kah-FWEE-leh*	the town is dead	Nyakyusa, Tanzania
Kajombo	*kah-JOM-boh*	boot	Yao, Malawi
Kamangeni	*kah-man-GEH-nee*	seems to be related	Ngoni, Malawi
Kamau	*kah-MAH-oo*	quiet warrior	Kikuyu, Kenya
Kambuji	*kahm-BOO-jee*	goat	Ngoni, Malawi
Kamowa	*kah-MOH-wah*	beer	Ngoni, Malawi
Kampibe	*kahm-PEE-beh*	go and look	Ngoni, Malawi
Kamuliva	*KAH-moo-lee-vah*	lamentable	Nguni, S. Africa
Kamuzu	*KAH-moo-zoo*	medicinal	Nguni, S. Africa

Name	Pronunciation	Meaning	Language and Country
Kamwendo	*kahm-WEHN-doh*	leg	Ngoni, Malawi
Kanjuchi	*kahn-JOO-chee*	bee	Ngoni, Malawi
Kapeni	*kah-PEH-nee*	knife	Yao, Malawi
Kaphiri	*kap-PEE-ree*	hill	Ngoni, Malawi
Kasiya	*kah-SEE-yah*	departure	Ngoni, Malawi
Kawduka	*kaw-DOO-kah*	crib	Ngoni, Malawi
Kayode	*KAH-yoh-deh*	he brought joy	Yoruba, Nigeria
Kazemde	*kah-ZEHM-deh*	ambassador	Yao, Malawi
Keambiroiro	*keh-am-bee-ROH-ee-roh*	mountain of blackness	Kikuyu, Kenya
Keanjaho	*keh-an-JAH-hoh*	mountain of beans	Kikuyu, Kenya
Keanyandaarwa	*keh-ah-nee-yan-DAR-wah*	mountain of hides	Kikuyu, Kenya
Kefentse	*keh-FENT-seh*	conqueror	Tswana, Botswana
Kehinde*	*keh-HEEN-deh*	second born of twins	Yoruba, Nigeria
Kereenyaga	*keh-rehn-YAH-gah*	mountain of mystery [i.e., Mt. Kenya]	Kikuyu, Kenya
Khaldun	*khal-DOON*	eternal	Arabic, N. Africa

Name	Pronunciation	Meaning	Language and Country
Khalfani	*kahl-FAH-nee*	destined to rule	Swahili, E. Africa
Khalid	*KHAH-leed*	eternal	Arabic, E. Africa
Khamisi	*kah-MEE-see*	born on Thursday	Swahili, E. Africa
Kifimbo*	*kee-FEEM-boh*	a very thin baby [*lit.* twig]	Swahili, E. Africa
Kigongo	*kee-GOHN-goh*	born before twins	Luganda, Uganda
Kitwana	*kee-TWAH-nah*	pledged to live	Swahili, E. Africa
Kizza	*keez-SAH*	born after twins	Luganda, Uganda
Kodwo	*koh-DWOH*	born on Monday	Twi, Ghana
Kofi	*koh-FEE*	born on Friday	Twi, Ghana
Kojo	*koh-JOH*	born on Monday	Akan, Ghana
Kokayi	*koh-KAH-yee*	summon the people	Shona, Zimbabwe
Kondo	*KON-doh*	war	Swahili, E. Africa
Kondwani	*kon-DWAH-nee*	joyful	Ngoni, Malawi
Kontar	*KOHN-tar*	only child	Akan, Ghana
Kopano	*koh-PAH-noh*	union	Tswana, S. Africa

Name	Pronunciation	Meaning	Language and Country
Kosoko	*koh-SOH-koh*	no hoe to dig a grave	Yoruba, Nigeria
Kpodo	*kpoh-DOH*	elder of twins	Ewe, Ghana
Kubweza	*koo-BWEH-zah*	give it back	Ngoni, Malawi
Kudyauku	*koo-YAH-oo-koo*	feast	Ngoni, Malawi
Kufuo	*koo-FOO-oh*	father shared birth pangs	Fante, Ghana
Kumanda	*koo-MAHN-dah*	graveyard	Ngoni, Malawi
Kunle	*KOON-leh*	home is filled with honors	Yoruba, Nigeria
Kuthakwakulu	*koo-tah-kwah-KOO-loo*	the end of man	Yao, Malawi
Kwabena	*KWAH-beh-nah*	born on Tuesday	Akan, Ghana
Kwacha	*KWAH-chah*	morning	Ngoni, Malawi
Kwada	*KWAH-dah*	night has fallen	Ngoni, Malawi
Kwakou	*kwah-KOO*	born on Wednesday	Ewe, Ghana
Kwame	*KWAH-meh*	born on Saturday	Akan, Ghana
Kwasi	*KWAH-see*	born on Sunday	Akan, Ghana
Kwayera	*kwah-YEH-rah*	dawn	Ngoni, Malawi

Name	Pronunciation	Meaning	Language and Country
Kwende	*KWEHN-deh*	let's go	Ngoni, Malawi
Lamburira	*lam-boo-REE-rah*	clean bush	Ngoni, Malawi
Lateef	*lah-TEEF*	gentle, pleasant	Arabic, N. Africa
Leabua	*LEH-ah-bwa*	you speak	Sotho, S. Africa
Letsego	*let-SEH-goh*	arm	Tswana, Botswana
Ligongo	*lee-GOHN-goh*	who is this?	Yao, Malawi
Linje	*LEEN-jeh*	try it	Yao, Malawi
Lipapwiche	*lee-pap-WEE-chay*	torn	Mwera, Kenya
Lisimba	*lee-SEEM-bah*	lion	Yao, Malawi
Liu	*LEE-oo*	voice	Ngoni, Malawi
Lizwelicha	*leez-weh-LEE-chah*	new world	Ndebele, Zimbabwe
Lugono	*loo-GOH-noh*	sleep	Ngoni, Malawi
Lukman	*look-MAHN*	prophet	Arabic, N. Africa
Lukongolo	*loo-KOHN-goh-loh*	leg	Yao, Malawi
Lumo	*LOO-moh*	born face downwards	Ewe, Ghana

Name	Pronunciation	Meaning	Language and Country
Lutalo	*LOO-tah-loh*	warrior	Luganda, Uganda
Luzige	*loo-zee-GHEH*	locust	Mugwere, Uganda
Machupa	*mah-CHOO-pah*	likes to drink	Swahili, E. Africa
Madaadi	*mah-DAH-dee*	name of an age-group	Kikuyu, Kenya
Madongo	*mah-DOHNG-goh*	uncircumcised	Luganda, Uganda
Madu	*MAH-doo*	people	Ibo, Nigeria
Madzimoyo	*mad-zee-MOH-yoh*	water of life	Ngoni, Malawi
Magomu	*mah-goh-MOO*	younger of twins	Luganda, Uganda
Maideyi	*mah-EE-deh-yee*	what did you want?	Shona, Zimbabwe
Makalani	*mah-kah-LAH-nee*	clerk, one skilled in writing	Mwera, Kenya
Makwangwala	*mah-kwan-GWAH-lah*	crown	Ngoni, Malawi
Malawa	*mah-LAH-wah*	flowers	Yao, Malawi
Mandala	*mahn-DAH-lah*	spectacles	Ngoni, Malawi
Mandondo	*mahn-DOHN-doh*	drops	Ngoni, Malawi
Manu	*mah-NOO*	the second born	Akan, Ghana

Name	Pronunciation	Meaning	Language and Country
Mapemba	*mah-PEHM-bah*	millet	Ngoni, Malawi
Mapira	*ma-PEE-rah*	millet	Yao, Malawi
Marwan	*mar-WAHN*	historical personage	Arabic, N. Africa
Masamba	*mah-SAHM-bah*	leaves	Yao, Malawi
Mashama	*mah-SHAH-mah*	you are surprised	Shona, Zimbabwe
Masibuwa	*mah-see-BOO-wah*	modern days	Yao, Malawi
Maskini	*mah-SKEE-nee*	poor	Swahili, Tanzania
Masomakali	*mah-soh-mah-KAH-lee*	sharp eyes	Nyakyusa, Tanzania
Masopakyindi	*mah-soh-pack-YEEN-dee*	eyes like hard porridge	Nyakyusa, Tanzania
Masud	*mah-SOOD*	fortunate	Swahili, E. Africa
Matsimela	*mat-see-MEH-lah*	roots	Sotho, Lesotho
Maulidi	*mah-oo-LEE-dee*	born during the Islamic month Maulidi	Swahili, E. Africa
Mawagali	*mah-wah-GAH-lee*	numerous	Abaluhya, Uganda
Mawulawde	*mah-woo-lah-weh-DAY*	God will provide	Ewe, Ghana
Mawuli	*MAH-woo-lee*	there is a God	Ewe, Ghana

Name	Pronunciation	Meaning	Language and Country
Mazi	*MAH-zee*	sir	Ibo, Nigeria
Mbita	*'m-BEE-tah*	born on a cold night	Swahili, E. Africa
Mbiya	*m-BEE-yah*	money	Yao, Malawi
Mbizi	*m-BEE-zee*	to drop in water	Lomwe, Malawi
Mbwana	*m-BWAH-nah*	master	Swahili, E. Africa
Mbwelera	*m-bweh-LEH-rah*	return	Ngoni, Malawi
Mensah	*MEN-sah*	third son	Ewe, Ghana
Mhina	*m-HEE-nah*	delightful	Swahili, E. Africa
Minkah	*MEEN-kah*	justice	Akan, Ghana
Mlengalenga	*m-leng-gah-LENG-gah*	heaven	Ngoni, Malawi
Modupe	*moh-DOO-peh*	thank you	Yoruba, Nigeria
Mongo	*MOHN-goh*	famous	Yoruba, Nigeria
Montsho	*MOHN-sho*	black	Tswana, Botswana
Mosegi	*moh-SEH-ghee*	tailor	Tswana, Botswana
Mosi*	*MOH-see*	first born	Swahili, Tanzania

Name	Pronunciation	Meaning	Language and Country
Moswen	*MOHSS-wehn*	light in color	Tswana, Botswana
Mothudi	*moh-TOO-dee*	smith	Tswana, Botswana
Motogusinile	*moh-toh-goo-see-NEE-leh*	the first is out	Nyakyusa, Tanzania
Moyenda	*moh-YEHN-dah*	on a journey	Ngoni, Malawi
Moyo	*MOH-yoh*	life, wellbeing, good health	Ngoni, Malawi
Mpasa	*'m-PAH-sah*	mat	Ngoni, Malawi
Mpenda	*'m-PEHN-dah*	lover, fond	Mwera, Kenya
Mpesi	*'m-PEH-see*	stock of maize	Ngoni, Malawi
Mposi	*'m-POH-see*	blacksmith	Nyakyusa, Tanzania
Mpumelele	*'m-poo-meh-LEH-loh*	success	Zulu, S. Africa
Msamaki	*'m-sah-MAH-kee*	like a fish	Swahili, Tanzania
Msrah	*'m-SRAH*	sixth born	Akan, Ghana
Mthuthuzeli	*'m-too-too-ZEH-lee*	comforter	Xhosa, S. Africa
Mtima	*'m-TEE-mah*	heart	Ngoni, Malawi
Mtumwa	*'m-TOOM-wah*	pledged	Swahili, E. Africa

Name	Pronunciation	Meaning	Language and Country
Mtundu	*'m-TOON-doo*	people, community	Ngoni, Malawi
Muawiyah	*moo-ah-WEE-yah*	pertaining to the Ommayid dynasty	Arabic, N. Africa
Muchaneta	*moo-chah-NEH-tah*	you will get tired	Shona, Zimbabwe
Mudada	*moo-DAH-dah*	the provider	Shona, Zimbabwe
Muhammad	*moo-HAH-mahd*	praised	Swahili, E. Africa
Mukhwana	*moo-KWAH-nah*	born as a twin	Abaluhya, Uganda
Mulogo	*MOO-loh-goh*	a wizard	Musoga, Uganda
Munanire	*moo-nah-nee-REH*	has more than his share	Luganda, Uganda
Munyiga	*moon-YEE-gah*	one who presses others	Mukiga, Uganda
Musa*	*MOO-sah*	child [*cf.* Moses]	Swahili, E. Africa
Muslim	*MOO-slim*	believer	Arabic, N. Africa
Musoke	*moo-soh-KEH*	cannot be introduced	Muganda, Uganda
Mvula*	*'m-VOO-lah*	rain	Ngoni, Malawi
Mwai	*'m-WAH-ee*	good fortune	Ngoni, Malawi
Mwaka	*'m-WAH-kah*	born during the opening of the farming year (Nairuz)	Swahili, E. Africa

Name	Pronunciation	Meaning	Language and Country
Mwamba	*'m-WAM-bah*	strong	Nyakyusa, Tanzania
Mwanyambi	*'m-wan-YAM-bee*	bag	Nyakyusa, Tanzania
Mwanyisa	*'m-WAHN-yee-sah*	accept defeat	Shona, Zimbabwe
Mwendapole	*'m-wen-dah-POH-leh*	takes his time	Nyakyusa, Tanzania
Mwinyi	*'m-WEEN-yee*	king	Swahili, E. Africa
Mwinyimkuu	*'m-ween-yeem-KOO-oo*	great king	Zaramo, Tanzania
Mwita	*'m-WEE-tah*	the summoner	Swahili, E. Africa
Naeem	*nah-EEM*	benevolent	Arabic, N. Africa
Najja	*NAHJ-jah*	born after	Muganda, Uganda
Nakisisa	*nah-kee-SEE-sah*	child of the shadows	Muganda, Uganda
Nangila	*NAN-ghee-lah*	born while parents were travelling	Abaluhya, Uganda
Nangwaya	*nahn-GWAH-yah*	don't trifle with me	Mwera, Kenya
Nassor	*NAH-sohr*	victorious	Swahili, Tanzania
Ndale	*'n-DAH-leh*	trick	Ngoni, Malawi
Ndembo	*'n-DEHM-boh*	elephant	Yao, Malawi

Name	Pronunciation	Meaning	Language and Country
Ndweleifwa	*'n-dweh-leh-EEF-wah*	I came with morning	Nyakyusa, Tanzania
Ngolinga	*'n-goh-LEENG-gah*	cry-baby	Yao, Malawi
Ngombe	*'n-GOHM-beh*	cow	Yao, Malawi
Ngonepe	*'n-goh-NEH-poh*	repose	Nyakyusa, Tanzania
Ngozi	*'n-GOH-zee*	blessing	Ibo, Nigeria
Ngunda	*'n-GOON-dah*	dove	Yao, Malawi
Nikusubila	*nee-koo-see-BEE-lah*	hopeful	Nyakyusa, Tanzania
Nizam	*nee-ZAHM*	discipliner, arranger	Arabic, N. Africa
Njete	*'n-JEH-teh*	salt	Yao, Malawi
Njowga	*'n-JOH-gah*	shoes	Mwera, Kenya
Nkosi	*'n-KOH-see*	ruler	Zulu, S. Africa
Nkrumah	*'n-KROO-mah*	ninth born	Akan, Ghana
Nkuku	*'n-koo-koo*	rooster	Yao, Malawi
Nkundinshuti	*'n-koon-deen-SHOO-tee*	convivial (*lit.* I like friends]	Rwanda, Rwanda
Nmeregini	*'n-MEH-reh-ghee-nee*	what have I done?	Ibo, Nigeria

Name	Pronunciation	Meaning	Language and Country
N'Namdi	*'n-NAHM-dee*	father's name lives on	Ibo, Nigeria
N'Nanna	*'n-NAHN-nah*	grandfather	Ibo, Nigeria
Nolizwe	*noh-leez-WEH*	country	Xhosa, S. Africa
Nonceba	*nong-CHEH-bah*	mercy	Xhosa, S. Africa
Nosakhere	*noh-SAH-keh-reh*	God's way is the only way	Benin, Nigeria
Nsoah	*'n-soh-AH*	seventh born	Akan, Ghana
Nsomba	*'n-SOHM-bah*	fish	Yao, Malawi
Nuru	*NOO-roo*	born in daylight	Swahili, E. Africa
Nwabudike	*NWAH-boo-dee-KEH*	son is the father's power	Ibo, Nigeria
Nyamekye*	*'n-yah-MEH-kee-eh*	God's gift	Akan, Ghana
Nyatui	*'n-YA-too-ee*	tiger fighter	Abaluhya, Uganda
Nyemba	*'n-YEM-bah*	beans	Ngoni, Malawi
Nyillingondo	*nee-yee-leen-GOHN-do*	handsome	Rwanda, Rwanda
Oba	*AW-bah*	king	Yoruba, Nigeria
Obadele	*aw-bah-DEH-leh*	the king arrives at the house	Yoruba, Nigeria

Name	Pronunciation	Meaning	Language and Country
Obafemi	*aw-bah-FEH-mee*	the king likes me	Yoruba, Nigeria
Obahnjoko	*aw-ban-JOH-koh*	the king is enthroned	Yoruba, Nigeria
Obaseki	*aw-BAH-seh-kee*	the king's influence goes beyond the market	Benin, Nigeria
Obataiye	*aw-bah-TAH-ee-yeh*	king of the world	Yoruba, Nigeria
Obawole	*aw-bah-WOH-leh*	the king enters the house	Yoruba, Nigeria
Obayana	*aw-bah-YAH-nah*	the king warms himself at the fire	Yoruba, Nigeria
Ochieng	*OH-chee-eng*	born in the daytime	Luo, Uganda
Ode	*oh-DEH*	one born along the road	Benin, Nigeria
Odimkemelu	*oh-deem-KEH-meh-loo*	I have done nothing wrong	Ibo, Nigeria
Odion	*OH-dee-ohm*	first of twins	Benin, Nigeria
Ogbonna	*oh-BOHN-nah*	image of his father	Ibo, Nigeria
Ogonna	*oh-GOH-nah*	father-in-law	Ibo, Nigeria
Ogunkeye	*oh-GOON-keh-yeh*	the god Ogun has gathered honor	Yoruba, Nigeria
Ogunsanwo	*oh-GOON-shahn-wo*	help comes from Ogun, god of war	Yoruba, Nigeria
Ogunsheye	*oh-GOON-sheh-yeh*	the god Ogun had acted honorably	Yoruba, Nigeria

Name	Pronunciation	Meaning	Language and Country
Ogwambi	*oh-GWAHM-bee*	always unfortunate	Luganda, Uganda
Ojo	*oh-JOH*	a difficult delivery	Yoruba, Nigeria
Ojore	*oh-joh-REH*	a man of war	Ateso, Uganda
Okafor*	*oh-KAH-for*	born on Afor market day	Ibo, Nigeria
Okanlawon	*oh-kahn-LAH-wohn*	son born after several daughters	Yoruba, Nigeria
Okechuku*	*oh-keh-CHOO-koo*	God's gift [*cf.* English: Theodore]	Ibo, Nigeria
Okeke	*oh-KEH-keh*	born on the market day	Ibo, Nigeria
Oko	*oh-KOH*	elder of twins	Ga, Ghana
Okonkwo*	*oh-KOHNG-kwoh*	born on Nkwo market day	Ibo, Nigeria
Okorie	*oh-KOH-ree-eh*	born on Oryo market day	Ibo, Nigeria
Okoth	*oh-KOTH*	born when it was raining	Luo, Uganda
Okpara	*ok-PAH-rah*	first son	Ibo, Nigeria
Ola	*AW-lah*	wealth, riches	Yoruba, Nigeria
Oladele	*aw-lah-DEH-leh*	honors, wealth arrive at home	Yoruba, Nigeria
Olafemi	*aw-lah-FEH-mee*	wealth, honor favors me	Yoruba, Nigeria

Name	Pronunciation	Meaning	Language and Country
Olamina	*aw-lah-MEE-nah*	this is my wealth	Yoruba, Nigeria
Olaniyan	*aw-lah-NEE-yahn*	honors surround me	Yoruba, Nigeria
Olatunji	*aw-lah-TOON-jee*	honor reawakens	Yoruba, Nigeria
Olu	*OH-loo*	pre-eminent	Yoruba, Nigeria
Olubayo	*oh-loo-BAH-yoh*	highest joy	Yoruba, Nigeria
Olufemi	*oh-loo-FEH-mee*	God loves me	Yoruba, Nigeria
Olugbala	*oh-LOO-bah-lah*	savior of the people	Yoruba, Nigeria
Olugbodi	*oh-LOO-boh-dee*	child born with supernumerary finger or toe	Yoruba, Nigeria
Olujimi	*oh-loo-JEE-mee*	God gave me this	Yoruba, Nigeria
Olukayode	*oh-loo-KAH-yoh-deh*	my lord brings happiness	Yoruba, Nigeria
Olumide	*oh-loo-MEE-deh*	my lord arrives	Yoruba, Nigeria
Olumiji	*oh-loo-MEE-jee*	my lord awakens	Yoruba, Nigeria
Oluoch	*oh-loo-OHCH*	born on a cloudy day	Luo, Ghana
Olushegun	*oh-loo-SHEH-goon*	God is the victor	Yoruba, Nigeria
Olushola	*oh-LOO-shoh-lah*	God has blessed me	Yoruba, Nigeria

Name	Pronunciation	Meaning	Language and Country
Olutosin	*oh-loo-TOH-seen*	God deserves to be praised	Yoruba, Nigeria
Oluwa	*oh-LOO-wah*	our lord	Yoruba, Nigeria
Oluyemi	*oh-loo-YEH-mee*	fulfillment from God	Yoruba, Nigeria
Omar	*OH-mar*	the highest [one of the Khalifah, followers of Muhammad]	Arabic, N. Africa
Omari	*oh-MAH-ree*	the highest	Swahili, E. Africa
Omolara	*oh-MOHN-lah-rah*	child born at the right time	Benin, Nigeria
Omorede	*oh-moh-REH-deh*	prince	Benin, Nigeria
Omoruyi	*oh-moh-ROO-yee*	respect from God	Benin, Nigeria
Omotunde	*oh-moh-TOON-deh*	a child comes again	Yoruba, Nigeria
Omwokha	*ohm-WOH-kah*	second of twins	Benin, Nigeria
Onani	*oh-NAH-nee*	look	Ngoni, Malawi
Onipede	*oh-nee-PEH-deh*	the consoler will come	Yoruba, Nigeria
Onuwachi	*oh-noo-WAH-chee*	God's world	Ibo, Nigeria
Onyebuchi	*on-yeh-BOO-chee*	who is God	Ibo, Nigeria
Onyemachi	*on-yeh-MAH-chi*	who knows God's will	Ibo, Nigeria

Name	Pronunciation	Meaning	Language and Country
Orji	*OR-jee*	mighty tree	Ibo, Nigeria
Osagboro	*oh-SAH-boh-roh*	there is only one God	Benin, Nigeria
Osahar	*oh-SAH-har*	God hears	Benin, Nigeria
Osakwe	*oh-SAH-kweh*	God agrees	Benin, Nigeria
Osayaba	*oh-sah-YAH-bah*	God forgives	Benin, Nigeria
Osayande	*oh-sah-YAHN-deh*	God owns the world	Benin, Nigeria
Osayimwese	*oh-sah-eem-WEH-seh*	God made me whole	Benin, Nigeria
Osaze	*oh-SAH-zeh*	whom God likes	Benin, Nigeria
Osei	*oh-SEH-ee*	noble	Fante, Ghana
Othiamba	*oh-tee-ahm-BAH*	born in the afternoon	Luo, Uganda
Othieno	*oh-tee-EH-noh*	born at night	Luo, Uganda
Ottah	*ot-TAH*	child thin at birth	Urhobo, Nigeria
Ouma	*oh-oo-MAH*	born through Caesarian surgery	Luo, Uganda
Owodunni	*oh-woh-DOON-nee*	it is nice to have money	Yoruba, Nigeria
Paki	*PAH-kee*	witness	Xhosa, S. Africa

Name	Pronunciation	Meaning	Language and Country
Paradzanai	*pah-rah-zah-NAH-ee*	keep it aside	Shona, Zimbabwe
Pepukayi	*peh-poo-KAH-yee*	wake up	Shona, Zimbabwe
Petiri	*PEH-tee-ree*	where we are	Shona, Zimbabwe
Peyisai	*peh-yee-SAH-ee*	conclusion	Shona, Zimbabwe
Pili	*PEE-lee*	the second born	Swahili, E. Africa
Quaashie	*kwah-SHEE*	born on Sunday	Ewe, Ghana
Rajabu	*rah-JAH-boo*	born in the Muslim seventh month	Swahili, E. Africa
Ramadhani	*rah-mah-DHAH-nee*	born during the month of Ramadan	Swahili, E. Africa
Rashidi	*rah-SHEE-dee*	of good council	Swahili, E. Africa
Roozani	*roh-ZAH-nee*	trick	Ngoni, Malawi
Rudo	*ROO-doh*	love	Shona, Zimbabwe
Runako	*roo-NAH-koh*	handsome	Shona, Zimbabwe
Runihura	*roo-nee-HOO-rah*	one who smashes to bits	Rwanda, Rwanda
Sabola	*sah-BOH-lah*	pepper	Ngoni, Malawi
Sadiki	*sah-DEE-kee*	faithful	Swahili, E. Africa

Name	Pronunciation	Meaning	Language and Country
Saeed	*sah-EED*	happy, fortunate	Arabic, N. Africa
Salehe	*sah-LEH-he*	good	Swahili, E. Africa
Salih	*SAH-lee*	good, right, proper	Arabic, N. Africa
Salim	*sah-LEEM*	peace	Swahili, E. Africa
Sebahive	*seh-bah-HEE-veh*	bringer of good fortune	Rwanda, Rwanda
Sefu	*SEH-foo*	sword	Swahili, E. Africa
Sekani	*seh-KAH-nee*	laughter	Ngoni, Malawi
Sekayi	*seh-KAH-yee*	laughter	Shona, Zimbabwe
Sentwali	*sehn-TWAH-lee*	brave one	Rwanda, Rwanda
Shaaboni	*shah-BOH-nee*	born in the eighth Muslim month	Swahili, E. Africa
Shakir	*SHAH-keer*	thankful	Arabic, N. Africa
Shangobunni	*shang-goh-BOON-nee*	a child given by Shango	Yoruba, Nigeria
Shawki	*SHAH-oo-kee*	yearning for right conduct	Arabic, N. Africa
Shomari	*shoh-MAH-ree*	forceful	Swahili, E. Africa
Shuaib	*shoo-AH-eeb*	Qur'anic prophet	Arabic, N. Africa

Name	Pronunciation	Meaning	Language and Country
Sifiye	*see-fee-YEH*	we are dying	Ndebele, Zimbabwe
Sigidi	*see-GHEE-dee*	a thousand	Zulu, S. Africa
Simba	*SEEM-bah*	lion [*cf.* Leo]	Swahili, E. Africa
Sipho	*see-POH*	gift	Zulu, S. Africa
Sipliwo	*see-PLEE-woh*	gift	Xhosa, S. Africa
Sisi	*see-SEE*	born on a Sunday	Fante, Ghana
Siwatu*	*see-WAH-too*	born during a time of conflict [*lit.* they are not people]	Swahili, E. Africa
Siwazuri	*see-wah-ZOO-ree*	they are not nice people	Swahili, E. Africa
Siyani	*see-YAH-nee*	relinquish	Ngoni, Malawi
Siyazini	*see-YAH-zee-nee*	what do we know?	Ndebele, Zimbabwe
Sowande	*shoh-WAHN-deh*	the wise healer sought me out	Yoruba, Nigeria
Sudi*	*SOO-dee*	luck	Swahili, E. Africa
Suhail	*soo-HAH-eel*	gentle, easy	Arabic, N. Africa
Suhuba	*soo-HOO-bah*	friend	Swahili, Tanzania
Sulaiman	*soo-lah-ee-MAHN*	peaceful [*cf.* Hebrew: Shelomon, Solomon]	Arabic, N. Africa

Name	Pronunciation	Meaning	Language and Country
Sultan	*sool–TAHN*	ruler	Swahili, E. Africa
Sundai	*soon–DAH–ee*	to push	Shona, Zimbabwe
Tabari	*TAH–bah–ree*	famous Muslim historian	Arabic, N. Africa
Tahir	*TAH–heer*	clean, pure	Arabic, N. Africa
Taiwo*	*TAH–ee–woh*	first born of twins	Yoruba, Nigeria
Tale	*TAH–leh*	green	Tswana, Botswana
Talib	*TAH–lib*	seeker	Arabic, N. Africa
Tarik	*TAH–rick*	Muslim general who conquered Spain	Arabic, N. Africa
Tau	*TAH–oo*	lion	Tswana, Botswana
Tebogo	*teh–BOH–goh*	gratitude	Tswana, Botswana
Teremun	*TEH–reh–moon*	father's acceptance	Tiv, Nigeria
Thabit	*TAH–bit*	firm	Arabic, N. Africa
Thabiti	*thah–BEE–tee*	a true man	Mwera, Kenya
Thako	*TAH–koh*	hip	Ngoni, Malawi
Thambo	*TAHM–boh*	ground	Ngoni, Malawi

Name	Pronunciation	Meaning	Language and Country
Thandiwe	*tahn-DEE-weh*	beloved	Zulu, S. Africa
Themba	*TEHM-bah*	hope	Xhosa, S. Africa
Thenga	*TEHNG-gah*	bring him	Yao, Malawi
Tichawonna	*tee-CHAH-oh-nah*	we shall see	Shona, Zimbabwe
Tor	*toor*	king	Tiv, Nigeria
Tsalani	*tsah-LAH-nee*	goodbye	Ngoni, Malawi
Tse	*tseh*	younger of twins	Ewe, Ghana
Tsekani	*tseh-KAH-nee*	close	Ngoni, Malawi
Tsoka	*TSOH-ka*	unlucky	Ngoni, Malawi
Tuako	*twah-KOH*	eleventh born	Ga, Ghana
Tukupasya	*too-koo-PASS-ya*	we are afraid	Nyakyusa, Tanzania
Tumaini	*too-MAH-ee-nee*	hope	Mwera, Kenya
Tuponile	*too-poh-NEE-leh*	we are saved	Nyakyusa, Tanzania
Tuwile	*too-WEE-leh*	death is inevitable	Mwera, Kenya
Twia	*TWEE-ah*	born after twins	Fante, Ghana

Name	Pronunciation	Meaning	Language and Country
Tyehimba	*tah-ee-heem-BAH*	we stand as a nation	Tiv, Nigeria
Ubaid	*oo-BAH-eed*	faithful	Arabic, N. Africa
Uche	*oo-CHEH*	thought	Ibo, Nigeria
Ufa	*OO-fah*	flour	Ngoni, Malawi
Umi	*OO-mee*	life	Yao, Malawi
Unika	*oo-NEE-kah*	light up	Lomwe, Malawi
Useni	*oo-SEH-nee*	tell me	Yao, Malawi
Usi	*OO-see*	smoke	Yao, Malawi
Usiku	*oo-SEE-koo*	night	Ngoni, Malawi
Uthman	*oot-MAHN*	one of the companions of the Prophet	Arabic, N. Africa
Uuka	*oo-OO-kah*	wake up	Xhosa, S. Africa
Vuai	*voo-AH-ee*	savior	Swahili, E. Africa
Wafor	*WAH-for*	born on Afor market day	Ibo, Nigeria
Waleed	*WAH-leed*	new born	Arabic, N. Africa
Wamukota	*WAH-moo-koh-tah*	left-handed	Abaluhya, Uganda

Name	Pronunciation	Meaning	Language and Country
Watende	*wah-TEHN-deh*	there shall be no revenge	Nyakyusa, Tanzania
Weke	*WEH-keh*	born on Eke market day	Ibo, Nigeria
Wemusa	*weh-moo-SAH*	never satisfied with his possessions	Luganda, Uganda
Worie	*WOH-ree-eh*	born on Afor market day	Ibo, Nigeria
Yafeu	*yah-FEH-oh*	bold	Fante, Ghana
Yahya	*YAH-yah*	God's gift	Swahili, E. Africa
Yao	*YAH-oh*	born on Thursday	Ewe, Ghana
Yawo	*YAH-woh*	born on a Thursday	Akan, Ghana
Yazid	*YAH-zid*	ever increasing	Arabic, N. Africa
Yohance	*Yoh-HAHN-seh*	God's gift [*cf.* John]	Hausa, Nigeria
Yoofi	*yoh-oh-FEE*	born on Friday	Akan, Ghana
Yooku	*yoh-oh-KOO*	born on Wednesday	Fante, Ghana
Yorkoo	*yor-KOH-oh*	born on Thursday	Fante, Ghana
Yusuf *	*yoo-SOOF*	he shall add (to his powers) [*cf.* Hebrew]	Swahili, E. Africa
Zahur	*zah-HOOR*	flower	Swahili, E. Africa

Name	Pronunciation	Meaning	Language and Country
Zaid	*ZAH-ee-id*	increase, growth	Arabic, N. Africa
Zesiro	*zeh-SEE-roh*	elder of twins	Luganda, Uganda
Zikomo	*zee-KOH-moh*	thank you	Ngoni, Malawi
Zilabamuzale	*zee-lah-bah-moo-ZAH-leh*	sickly child	Luganda, Uganda
Ziyad	*zee-YAHD*	an increase	Arabic, N. Africa
Zuberi	*zoo-BEH-ree*	strong	Swahili, E. Africa
Zuka	*zoo-KAH*	sixpence	Shona, Zimbabwe

Commentary

In Africa the naming of a child is a matter of great importance. A number of considerations influence the choice of the name or names to be given. Was the child born in the morning, in the evening, or at night? On what weekday or market-day was he born? What special circumstances relating to the child himself, to his parents, to the extended family, or to the national community attended his birth? Is this the parents' first child, or first female child? Is the child one of twins, and if so, is it the elder or the younger and are the twins a boy and a girl or are they of the same sex?

The Yoruba people of Nigeria have a saying: "We consider the state of our affairs before we name a child." This attitude is general throughout Africa, and so, since Africans are extremely fond of children a birth in the family is, as a rule, an occasion for rejoicing. Indeed, the child is very often given a name which precisely refers to the family's happiness in welcoming the newcomer. Thus the Nyakyusa people of Tanzania might name a baby girl *Sekelaga* "Rejoice," or *Tusajigwe* "We are blessed." The Swahili-speaking people of the same country might make a similar if somewhat less expansive communication by naming a new baby boy *Sudi* "Luck." In the same way, the Akan people of Ghana will name the new arrival, if it is male, *Nyamekye* "Gift of God," a sentiment also expressed among the Ibo people of Nigeria in the boy's name *Okechuku*.

The joy and hope, and even the anxious fears of the parents for the child's wellbeing can be expressed and made memorable through the name given to the child. Generally speaking, however, the coming of a child is seen within African society as a happy and fortunate occurrence, a landmark in the life of the family and a significant incident in the collective existence of the community. Africans are very religious; thus a family may through the name given to a child be saying that they consider the child's coming as a mark of divine favor, a blessing duly acknowledged in a boy's name such as *Chukwueneka* "God has dealt kindly with us" (Ibo, Nigeria), or in the girl's name *Sibongile*, which simply says "Thanks" (Ndebele, Zimbabwe).

Some African names indicate an event, natural or otherwise, that took place around the time of the child's birth. Thus an Ngoni male child might be named *Mvula* "Rain" because such a precipitation occurred around the time he was born. A child born to Swahili-speaking parents during a time of trouble might be given the name *Taabu*. The influence of the Muslim religion has been profound in Africa, and Islam has been so Africanized that it has long ago in many areas ceased to be regarded as anything other than an African religion. Naturally, then, children are given by Muslim parents names which are in fact Arabic names, associated with the Muslim religion.

Ceremonies associated with the naming of a child differ from place to place in Africa. Nevertheless there are certain features which appear rather consistently in one form or another over the continent. Particularly is this true of the purpose of the formal bestowing of the name, for in African societies generally the name conferred on the new-born is not merely to distinguish the individual child, but—more importantly—to acknowledge and welcome the newcomer as a member of the community, to congratulate the parents, and to make auspicious predictions for the child's future.

Indeed it is not until a child has been named that he is considered a person; and a name is not given until it has been agreed that the child has come to stay. This is in implicit recognition of the unfortunate fact of high infant mortality in many areas. Thus, until the child is formally named it is referred to by no other term but "it" or "thing." Sometimes, perhaps because the child although surviving remains of doubtful viability, the "it" characterization sticks. So it is that the Ngoni name *Chabwera* "He has arrived" is, in fact, more precisely "it has arrived." In some instances there are two namings: the first is a trial naming, pending the decision that the child will stay, while the second confers on the child the name he is to bear for life. The first name given may be quite uncomplimentary, for instance "I am dead" or "I am ugly"; in this way it is hoped to avoid the jealousy of the ancestors who might wish to take back to themselves a child who is born especially healthy or good-looking. The final naming, however, may be regarded as completing the act of birth. If, then, the child dies before his real-life name is given, he is regarded as not having been born at all, or having been still-born. Most Africans hold that it is only an individual's body that can die, and that the spirit lives on, inhabiting many bodies in many lifetimes.

76

The occurrence of a still-birth or a death before naming is regarded as indicating that for some reason no spirit chose to utilize the body prepared by the expectant parents. In such a case, the parents entertain the hope and expectation that the family member seeking rebirth will return to occupy a body provided by them in a subsequent conception.

The naming of a child, then, has as its purpose the recognition of a new personal presence incarnate within the community. The ceremonies and customs associated with birth lead the child normally and naturally to his absorption into the community in which he will ultimately, as an adult, find his personal fulfilment through his active functioning in the total society. Symbolic of the close relationship of the young child to his mother and of his subsequent separation from her into the society at large is the special treatment given to the placenta and umbilical cord in most African societies. Whether the placenta is carefully buried and the burial-place invested with special significance for the child or whether it is unceremoniously discarded, common to both actions is the notion of the child's impending separation from the maternal nurture and protection. It is as a rule after the falling off of the umbilical cord that the child is considered ready to be formally named. The Ndebele bury the umbilical cord and placenta right under the floor of the house in which the birth took place, and thence the paradox ensues that, as J. S. Mbiti has expressed it, "The child is near the mother and yet begins to get away from the individual mother, growing into the status of being 'I am because we are, and since we are therefore I am.' "

Another important aspect of the naming ceremony to be observed throughout Africa is the role of the aged. Indeed the very young and the very old are regarded as being very closely related experientially since the infant is seen as but recently returned from where the aged is preparing to go. In a number of instances it is an aged midwife who ritually attends the child and finally hands it to its mother after it has been named. It is an elderly person who whispers the child's name into its ears before announcing it to the crowd (the baby should be the first to know its own name!) and, after an appropriate prayer, spits in the child's ear to fix the name in its head. The giving of gifts is often a feature of the ceremony (in some instances African etiquette prescribing that women present their gifts to the mother, and men theirs to the father).

The occasion of the naming ceremony is one of rejoicing, with feasting and dancing. The ceremony brings together the oldest in the community—the elders—and the youngest—the new-born, newly named child. And in these encounters across the years the continuity of a people's life is ritually reaffirmed, and witnessed in actuality. The naming ceremony is also a profoundly religious occasion. The invocation of divinity, the sense of the ancestors' interest and involvement, the prayers and blessings, are all part of a communal religious experience of which the child serves as a focus.

The overwhelming majority of African names are either single words or a number of words combined into a phrase in the language of the child's family. Thus the Yoruba male and female name *Ayo* means "joy" in the Yoruba language, and the word is found in other names, as in the girl's name *Ayodele* "joy enters the home." In addition, however, to the names given to an individual as a baby, Africans take to themselves or have bestowed on them other names, with the result that a person one knew by a particular name five years ago might today be known by quite a different name, and brothers born of the same parents might have quite different names since in many societies there are no "family" names by which everyone in a given family may be identified.

Some names in this book are drawn from countries in East Africa—Tanzania, Uganda, Malawi, and Zimbabwe (also miscalled Rhodesia). Others are drawn from West African countries—Nigeria and Ghana. Yet others are taken from countries in Southern Africa—Botswana, Lesotho, and Azania (presently called South Africa). They are, it will be observed, only an illustrative sampling of African names. Ghana and Nigeria have a particular appeal for African-Americans, not only because many of their forebears came from West Africa, but also because of the inspiration that these countries gave to their transplanted brethren when they were the earliest African states to regain independence. In East Africa, Tanzania, and Zambia (which shares a cultural heritage with not-yet-liberated Zimbabwe) are of great importance in the continuing development of Pan-African consciousness, and Malawi has a rich historical and cultural heritage which is relatively uninvestigated. It will be useful, we dare say, to look more closely at some of these countries in respect of the names of individuals, their significance, and especially the ways in which naming customs can be illustrative of the life-style of an African community.

Yoruba, Nigeria

The Yoruba people name a male child on the ninth day, and a female child on the seventh day after birth. Twins are named on the eighth day after birth, as are Christian and Muslim children. Until a child is formally and ceremonially named it is never called by any significant name, but is referred to simply as *Ikoko Omon* which means "newborn child"; the mother is called *Iya Ikoko*, which means "mother of the newborn." It is at the time of the naming ceremony that the child for the first time will leave his home; at this time, too, the mother's confinement formally ends and she leaves the house for the first time after delivery.

The naming ceremony is held at the parents' house either early in the morning or in the early afternoon. Present are the child's grandparents, uncles, aunts, cousins, in-laws, and members of the community. Each person brings a gift which is left at the door of the house upon entering. The gift might be an article of clothing for the child or an item of use to the parents or the household in connection with the coming of the child. Female relatives and friends give their gifts to the child's mother, and males their gifts to the father. The room in which the ceremony is to be held is prepared for the occasion with festive decorations. In the center of the room are placed vessels containing water, red pepper, salt, oil, honey, liquor, and kola nuts. The mother enters from another room with the baby. She hands the child to an elderly person, usually a woman, and the naming ceremony is about to begin.

The baby is handed over to the elder who is to perform the rituals of the naming ceremony. Water is sprinkled toward the ceiling and some applied to the baby. If the child cries when the water touches him this is regarded with approval and satisfaction as an indication that the child has come to stay, since only living things can produce noise of their own accord. At this point the officiating elder whispers the child's name into its ear and then, dipping the tip of his finger into the water and with it touching the child's forehead, he announces the child's name to the assemblage. Now, turning to the vessels in the center of the room, the elder puts a little bit of pepper in the baby's mouth to symbolize that the baby will be resolute and have command over the forces of nature.

Water is next put into the child's mouth, symbolizing a wish for his purity of body and spirit and hence his freedom from disease. Then a little salt is put into his mouth, symbolizing the flavor of wisdom with which it is wished that he be divinely fed. Oil is next touched to his lips symbolizing the wish that he enjoy power and health like that of royalty. Honey, then liquor, are touched to his lips, the one signifying the happiness and the other the prosperity that are to be his. Finally the child is given a taste of kola nut, symbolic of the wish for his good fortune. Each one of the items, after having been first given to the baby to taste, is passed around for those present to taste.

The ritual over, the festivities begin. There is feasting and dancing lasting into the early hours of the next day. At times during these proceedings musicians sing songs of praise to the child, its parents, its relatives and friends. In these acts, a new member is being welcomed into the Yoruba community, a human being in his own right and known by his own name.

The complete appellation conferred on a Yoruba child in his naming ceremony usually consists in fact of three names. The first name is the *oruko*, or "personal" name. This name might be either an *oruko-amun-torun-wa* (name the child is "born with"), or an *abiso* name (name relating to the circumstances existing in the family at the time of his birth). The second name is the *oriki*, or "praise name," an attributive name which expresses what the child is, or is hoped to become. The third name is the *orile*, a name indicative of the child's kinship group's origin.

A child is considered as having been "born with" a name when he or she falls within a specific category, such as *ibeji* (twins). Thus the first-born (whether male or female) of twins is, by tradition, called *Taiwo*, a name derived from a phrase (*to-aye-wo*) which means "tasted the world." The second-born of twins, whether male or female, is given the name *Kehinde*. There are several of these "born with" categories. Another example is the category into which a child falls if he is considered to be the reincarnation of a grandparent. (This judgement is arrived at on the basis of certain marks on the body of the child by which the particular individual being reincarnated is recognized.) A male child considered to be the reincarnation of his grandfather is named *Babatunde* ("father has returned"), and a female child judged to be her grandmother reborn is given the name *Yetunde* ("mother has returned").

As distinct from the *amun-torun-wa*, the name the child is "born with," the child's first name or *oruko* may be an *abiso* name. If a child does not fall into a category which automatically confers on him a name, a parent or grandparent or any elderly member of the family may give him an *abiso* name. (A child may, on occasion, end up with two or three *abiso* names.) In keeping with the Yoruba saying *ile la i wo ka to so omon loruko* "we consider the state of our affairs before we name our child," the *abiso* name is framed to refer to family circumstances prevailing at the time of the child's birth. Thus a family which has for a long time been wishing for a baby might name the new arrival *Ayodele* "joy enters the home."

As mentioned above, the name following the first name is the *oriki*. Whereas the *oruko* is either the name the child was "born with" or refers to the family circumstances at the time of his birth, the *oriki*, or "praise name" is complimentary to the child. The *oriki* of a male child has an heroic connotation, for example, *Ajamu* "he fights for what he wants." On the other hand, the *oriki* of a female child expresses endearment, thus *Jumoke* means "everybody loves this child."

The third name of a Yoruba child, the *orile*, relates, as we noted before, to the kinship group lineage traced as far back as possible, to the earliest progenitor, such often being a specific legendary hero or divinity such as *Ogun*, the god of war. The sense of kinship and group continuity may also be expressed in a name relating to an animal or plant or object held sacred by the group of families tracing their origin to a common ancestor.

It is possible therefore to designate an individual very clearly by stating his full name, that is, his *oruko* + *oriki* + *orile*. The conversion to Islam or Christianity of some Yorubas has on occasion caused the *oruko* name to be displaced by a Muslim or Christian name such as Alihu or Samuel. In such cases the *abiso* and *orile* are dropped and the *oruko* remains as a "surname." We may leave further discussion of this subject since our purpose is to deal with naming according to the indigenous African condition.

81

Ibo, Nigeria

The Yoruba way of naming children has been dealt with rather extensively in the foregoing, but other African, or West African, or even more closely, Nigerian peoples are not lacking in a rich onomastic heritage. The fact is rather that purely linguistic features (affecting the "shape," sound, and meaning of the names) apart, fundamental considerations and attitudes relating to the naming of children exhibit striking similarities. As a general rule, African children are prized and treated as welcome guests in the home, favored with much affection, and their coming to a family is regarded and celebrated as an occasion for communal jubilation. And this love of children is universally to be observed in the names the children bear. Thus even the quite uncomplimentary name *Chotsani* "take it away" (Yao, Malawi) is not in fact an expression of rejection but rather an attempt by the family to conceal or disguise its joy so that the divinities or the ancestors will not take back the precious infant. Thus, among the Ibo, another Nigerian people, the name of the child is also not a mere label by which an individual is to be distinguished from others, but is a memento of a distinction, of an event, or of circumstances related to the life of the family or of the community.

An Ibo child is given several names. The choice of names is based on judgements and observations concerning the child, such as its health or birthmarks on its body, or some remarkable characteristic. Another factor in the choice of name could be the opinion of a diviner who might associate the child with a particular divinity.

An Ibo child may also be named after the market day on which he was born. Thus a boy with the name *Okonkwo* shows by that name that he was born on the Nkwo market day. (Similarly *Okafor* was born on the Afor market day.)

Hausa, Nigeria

The Hausa are a Muslim people in Nigeria. Every Hausa child, then, has a Muslim name. In addition he has a nickname referring to an object, a physical trait of his, the sequence in which he was born, or an event coinciding with the time of his birth. The nickname may also be expressive of wishes for his good health and fortune. Another name which is, in fact, a laudatory title may be bestowed on a Hausa person; and somewhat similar to this is a nickname automatically borne by an individual having the name of a Muslim notable of the past. Accordingly Hausa male children are given names like *Musa* (Moses), *Dauda* (David), *Yusuf* (Joseph), *Alhasan* and *Mamadu*. Female children are given names like *Hawa* (Eve), *Hasana* ("good") and *Zainabu* ("beautiful").

Hausa nicknames are very allusive. A girl with the given name *Bilqisu* automatically bears the nickname *Gado*, in reference to the throne (*gado*) on which Belkis, Queen of Sheba, is said to have been seated when King Solomon paid her a visit in her apartments during her stay in Jerusalem. So also a boy, *Ibrahim* by given name, will have the nickname *Cigari* ("Town-conqueror") since a former Ibrahim, King of Kano, bore that nickname. The Hausas also have names denoting twins, and a child whose mother or father died soon after his or her birth is recognized in that characterisation by the nickname *Talle*.

Akan, Ghana

Akan, spoken in Ghana, is a language of the Kwa group of West Africa. Sister languages to Akan are Ewe, Ga, and Twi, also spoken in Ghana. Ashanti and Fante are forms of Akan. It is because of this linguistic relationship and also because of the important role of the Akan peoples in the history and culture of Ghana that it is convenient to discuss names in Ghana under the general heading *Akan*, since these names and the notions associated with them are quite similar and in many instances identical.

A Ghanaian is taught from his infancy that the name he bears was not lightly given to him and that his actions must therefore be such as will bring honor to the name. A proverb which conveys this message instructs: "A great name is the title only of men of noble deeds."

To be named after a distinguished person invests the individual with the responsibility to emulate in his own life the character of the individual whose name he bears.

83

A Ghanaian name has two parts, the soul's name (*Akeradini*) and the name given by the father to his child (the *Agyadini*). The first name is that of the deity associated with the day on which the child was born. The name is not considered as being a name *given* to the child; it is seen rather, as with the Yorubas, as the name the child was "born with," and cannot be changed at will. The *Akeradini* is actually conferred at the very hour of the child's birth, being declared and pronounced by the person who attends the mother at the time of delivery. The Ghanaian naming ceremony, called the *Adinto*, takes place early in the morning of the seventh day after the day on which the child was born. On this occasion the *Agyadini* (or *Abadini*) is conferred by the father, who chooses from among the main second names of distinguished relatives from his own father's family. The names, actually, fall into categories which are rather similar to those of the Yoruba *abiso* names.

Swahili, Kenya and Tanzania

Swahili is a basically Bantu language, spoken over an area of eastern and central Africa which embraces the countries of Tanzania, Kenya, Uganda, Rwanda, Burundi, and in the Congo the provinces of Katanga, Kivu, and Kinshasa, northern Malawi, northern Zambia, Mozambique, the northern and western parts of the Malagasy Republic, and the Comoro Islands. Swahili is the national language of Tanzania, Kenya, and the province of Katanga in the Congo, but is the first language of the majority of people of the East African coastal region. There are, in fact, several dialects of Swahili as a consequence of its wide territorial sweep. The speakers of Swahili dialects are, however, all mutually intelligible; and the dialect of Zanzibar, the "spice island" just off the East African coast, is the standard form. Swahili names, then, are to be found among people of a number of nationalities and ethnic groups in eastern and central Africa. Islam has for centuries been an important presence and influence in East Africa and indeed Arabic has made a considerable contribution to the Swahili vocabulary. In addition, then, to the Bantu-language names in Swahili, there are many names in the region that are in reality the Swahilized forms of Muslim, that is Arabic, names. Readily recognizable Muslim names in Swahili garb are

Abdulla (Abdullah), *Omari* (Omar) and *Huseni* (Hussein). Biblical names also used by Muslims may also be recognized in their Swahili form: *Musa* (Moses), *Daudi* (David), *Issa* (Joshua and also Jesus). Names that are pure Bantu are: *Kifimbo* ("stick"), *Mosi* ("first"), and *Siwatu* ("they are not people").

Among Swahili-speaking people a child is given a name immediately after birth. This is his *jina la utotoni* or "childhood name," and is given him by an elderly relative or on occasion by the midwife assisting the delivery. This is somewhat of the nature of a nickname and may either describe the circumstances at the time of the child's birth (*Chuki* means hatred), physical appearance (*Panya* means "mouse," i.e. tiny) or health (*Mwatabu* means "child of sorrow," referring as well to trouble in the family situation as difficulty in the birth itself.

Seven days after his birth (sometimes forty days after), the child is given his *jina la ukubwani*, his "adult name," usually of Islamic or Biblical origin, and always given by the child's parents or paternal grandparents. The eldest in a family, if a boy, usually bears the name of his paternal grandfather; if the eldest child is a girl, however, she is given the name of her paternal grandmother.

Ceremonies differ from place to place in Swahili-speaking countries, and even among different families within the same immediate area. They are in most cases along the same general lines, however, with the elders playing a significant role in the proceedings, and considerable attention being paid to the requirements of family and religious traditions.

Of particular interest in recent years is the re-adoption of African names by Afro-Americans. As has been noted above, it is rather common for Africans to discard one name and assume another considered more suitable. This is done, appropriately, when the individual concerned has acquired some special personal characteristic—physical, intellectual, or moral—or is perceived as being capable of displaying some distinctive quality of personality or achievement. In a very real sense, then, to Africans the name is the person, and African-Americans who replace their "Christian" names with African names are not only thereby claiming and expressing a right to intellectual, cultural and political self-determination, but are also, in this respect, acting in full accordance with ancestral precedent as well as contemporary African practice.

Thus the athlete Kareem Abdul-Jabbar (formerly Lew Alcindor) by his chosen name indicates his aspiration to or expression of the qualities of kindliness, religious devotion, and supreme courage. The name of the author and political activist Imamu Amiri Baraka (formerly LeRoi Jones) aptly distinguishes him as "a religious leader, noble and blessed (or gifted)." The illustrious Islamic names Muhammad ("praised") and Ali ("exalted") are combined in the chosen name of the world-renowned boxing champion Muhammad Ali (formerly Cassius Clay).

The name changes of these well-known Afro-American public figures, as of many others less well known, constitute in effect a conscious rejection of European names which are being perceived increasingly by Afro-Americans as but another form of psychological control imposed by an alien and most often hostile dominant society. At the same time, the careful consideration reflected in the apt description or self-fulfilling prophecy conveyed by the chosen names is clear evidence of the bearers' intent to be identified by names which signify their spiritual liberation and declare their proper personal and group identity.

As we have seen, in the African tradition, today as yesterday, a name is not a mere identification tag; it is a record of family and community history, a distinct personal reference, an indication of present status, and an enunciated promise of future accomplishment.

No wonder, then, that the Ghanaian sage Opanin Kwame Nyame declared:
"Man came to seek a name, and nothing more."

Keith E. Baird
New York, 1972

Editor's Acknowledgement

Thanks are due to a number of friends and colleagues who kindly placed themselves at my disposal for checking both the meaning and pronunciation of the names listed. Particularly, acknowledgement of assistance is due to Mr. Abamola James, Information Officer of the Consulate-General of Nigeria at New York City, for information on Yoruba names; to Dr. Francis Botchway of Richmond College, C.U.N.Y., for information on Ghanaian names; to Professor Sharifa Zawawi of City College, C.U.N.Y., for information on Arabic and Swahili names; and to my colleague at Hofstra University, Mr. D. Callistus Nkobi-Ndlovu, for information on names from Zanzibar and Southern Africa. Special thanks are rendered to Mrs. Brenda Biram of Johnson Publishing Company, who was always encouraging and helpful.

K.E.B.

Bibliographical Note

The following is a listing of works which have been useful in the preparation of this Commentary. Dealing specifically with African names are:

Hakim, Dawud. *Arabic Names and Other African Names with their Meanings*. Philadelphia: Hakim's Publications, 1970. The author provides a number of African names of Arabic as well as of indigenous origin from various parts of the continent. Pronunciation is given only for indigenous African names, since Muslims, for whom the work was apparently primarily written, might be presumed to be instructed in the language associated with their religion, and thus would not need to be given the pronunciation for the Arabic names.

Osuntoki, Chief. *The Book of African Names*. Washington: Drum and Spear Press, 1970. This book by a Nigerian, in addition to a listing of names from various regions of Africa, gives interesting information about naming ceremonies.

Two texts which do not deal specifically with names, one a dictionary, the other a teaching text, have been very informative.

Abraham, R. C. *Dictionary of Modern Yoruba*. London: University of London Press, 1958. This dictionary of the Yoruba language treats Yoruba names in both their linguistic and social contexts.

Zawawi, Sharifa. *Kiswahili kwa Kitendo*. New York: Harper & Row, 1971. This work is actually an excellent Swahili introductory course which includes in its Utangulizi (Introduction) a discussion on "Naming Children in Swahili."

Providing an important insight into the background of African traditional thought and custom within the conceptual context of which the naming of a child naturally takes place are:

Antubam, Kofi. *Ghana's Heritage of Culture*. Leipzig: Koehler & Amelang, 1963. This is a compendious work about Ghana's traditional culture by one of its greatest artists.

Mbiti, J. S. *African Religions and Philosophy*. New York: Praeger, 1969. As the name implies, this work deals with African belief systems, including both the traditional and those responding to the contemporary quest for new identity, values, and sanctions.

Uchendu, Victor C. *The Igbo of Southeast Nigeria*. New York: Holt, Rinehart & Winston, 1965. This work is a case study in cultural anthropology written about the Ibo culture by an Ibo. Its information on the names and naming ceremony, though necessarily brief, is authoritative.

Further sources which have proved helpful are:

Adefunmi, Baba Oseijeman. *African Names from the Ancient Yoruba Kingdom of Nigeria*. New York: The Yoruba Academy, n.d.

Black Names in Yoruba and Arabic. Brooklyn, N.Y.: ABC of Islam Publications, n.d.

Forum. Magazine of the African-American Teachers Association. February and March, 1971.

Sholola, Bandele. "More African Names: The Yoruba Way," in *African Progress*, Sept.–Oct., 1971.

Ogonna Chuks-orji   Keith E. Baird

Ogonna Chuks-orji was born on May 29, 1942 in Aba, a city of 350,000 people in the state of Nigeria, the second of his parents' ten children, of the Ibo people. He travelled widely in Africa, Asia, Europe, and the U.S.A. Mr. Chuks-orji has studied at the College of Marin, San Francisco State College, where he received a B.A. in 1968, and at the University of San Francisco Graduate School of Business (M.B.A., 1970), and is currently working toward a Ph.D. from the University of California. He is also executive director of Pan Africa House in San Francisco, an association of African and American students which has been in existence since 1962. The association serves as a cultural and information center for African students and their American friends.

Keith E. Baird was born in 1923 in Barbados, West Indies, and is a United States citizen. He is now professor of humanities at Hofstra University, New York, and was director of African and Afro-American History, Department of Black and Puerto Rican Studies, at Hunter College from 1968–69; director of African and Afro-American History and the Culture Center of N.Y.C. Board of Education from 1967–68, and is consultant in African and Afro-American History—Heritage Program for HARYOU-ACT, New York. He holds numerous other consultancies and has been active in many organizations concerned with African-American studies, linguistics, and writing. He speaks ten languages and has lectured at colleges and universities throughout the United States.

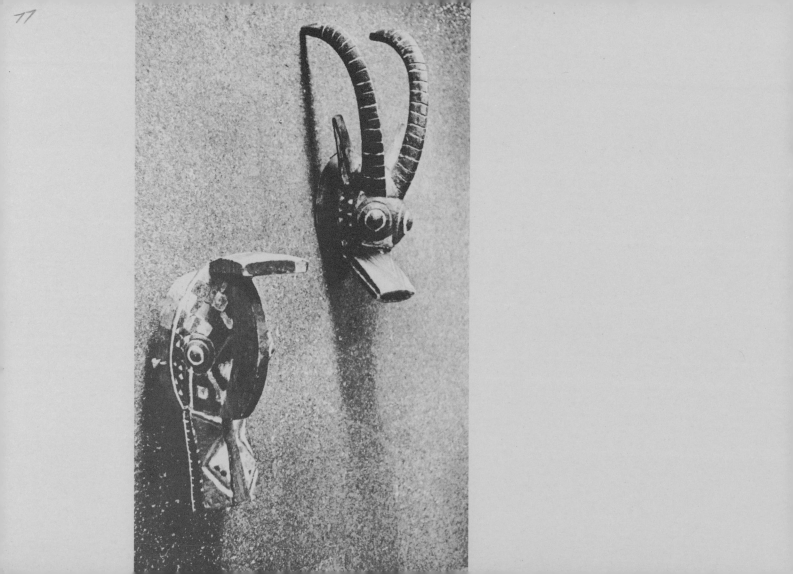